"If you are familiar with Charles Spurgeon's sermons, you will want to get a hold of these abridged 'sermonettes' drawn from those same sermons on texts related to Christmas. Pithy, pastoral, and pointed, this little book will give you a wonderful insight into the child lying in a manger—God in the flesh—and leave you in awe for many a Christmas."

Jonny Gibson, Minister, Tenth Presbyterian Church, Philadelphia; Author, *O Come, O Come, Emmanuel: A Liturgy for Daily Worship from Advent to Epiphany*

"Though we're approaching the 200th anniversary of his birth, Christians still cannot get enough of Charles Spurgeon. That's because the great preacher was biblically and theologically faithful, and his ministry impacted the world—and continues to do so to this day. Spurgeon's faithfulness and enduring relevance is why I'm delighted to recommend Jeff Medders' new book. In this encouraging work, Medders presents the best of Spurgeon on Advent texts and does so in an accessible, easy-to-read way. I encourage you to deepen and enrich your Christmas celebration by familiarizing yourself with this fine work."

Jason K. Allen, Ph.D., President, Midwestern Baptist Theological Seminary & Spurgeon College

"Jeff Medders has given the church a double gift with this Advent devotional. Not only has he mined the depths of Spurgeon's sermons for rich seasonal reflections, but he has carefully selected passages that beautifully showcase the glory of Jesus Christ. In a season when we long for our hearts to marvel afresh at the birth of Immanuel, this book will be a true blessing."

Emily Jensen, Coauthor, *Risen Motherhood and Gospel Mom*

"As we pull out the boxes of Christmas decorations, this book pulls out riches from Spurgeon's storehouses. These concise and Christ-centered daily devotions anchor the reader in Scripture amid a frantic, commercialized season. The 'Prince of Preachers' seems to speak directly to us: *Behold the newborn king!*"

Aimee Joseph, Author, *Midlife Plot Twist: Trusting God Through the Turbulence of Perimenopause*; Bible teacher

For Natalie,
whose name and heart
celebrate the birth of our Lord.

THE NEWBORN KING

C.H. SPURGEON

25 DEVOTIONS FOR ADVENT

EDITED BY
J.A. MEDDERS

thegoodbook
COMPANY

The Newborn King

Published by:
The Good Book Company

thegoodbook.com | thegoodbook.co.uk
thegoodbook.com.au | thegoodbook.co.nz

Every book published by The Good Book Company has been written by a human author and edited by a human editor. While AI tools are sometimes used to assist with research and support certain processes, all content has been created by a human author and thoroughly checked by our editorial team to ensure it is biblically faithful and pastorally wise.

Published in association with the literary agency of THE GATES GROUP.

Design by André Parker | Based on an original cover design by Faceout Studio

ISBN: 9781802544480 | JOB-008601 | Printed in India

CONTENTS

PREFACE

Charles Haddon Spurgeon (1834–1892), pastor of the Metropolitan Tabernacle in London, is known as one of the most beloved pastors, writers, and preachers in the history of Christ's church. It's not because his sermons and books have sold millions of copies worldwide or because he has had more words published in English than anyone else. And it's not because thousands were converted and baptized through his ministry or because he founded a college for pastors. Spurgeon is a soul-edifying read because his sermons overflow with the sweet aroma of Jesus Christ. His preaching was unparalleled in making known the glory of Christ. The grace of God is unavoidable in Spurgeon's works. Whatever the sermon, lecture, or book, Spurgeon exalted our great God and Savior. And this book is no different.

You are holding a new book from C.H. Spurgeon—at least, that's what I hope you will experience as you read. His famous devotionals—*Morning by Morning* and *Evening by Evening*—were created from summaries, excerpts, and outlines of his sermons. And it's in that same spirit that I pulled this book together from Spurgeon's sermons. When I realized that Spurgeon never created an Easter or Advent devotional, I knew one needed to be published—and it is my privilege to be a steward of Spurgeon's sermons in *The Risen King* (released in 2025) and *The Newborn King* (2026). I hope you will enjoy these books as though they are new works from the "Prince of Preachers."

I began this project by imagining what Spurgeon would have written and emphasized if he were the one writing. From my years of personal and doctoral work on Spurgeon, I have studied the vast catalog of his sermons and have selected texts and topics for the themes at hand. From these sermons, I pulled excerpts that showcase what many have come to love and expect from Spurgeon—piercing insights, vivid language, and soul-thrilling meditations on Christ's person and work. As I read sermon after sermon, I compiled entries from single or multiple sermons that fully capture Spurgeon's voice and insights on the biblical text and theme. While I did, gently and sparingly, modernize language and sentence structure at spots to better serve those new to Spurgeon and his Victorian English, I hope that my presence is minimal. As the editor, I have written a clarifying or summarizing sentence for context at some points, but, rest assured, you are reading Spurgeon.

As you read *The Newborn King* and journey through the Christmas narrative and connected doctrines during this Advent season, I hope and pray that Spurgeon's words will help you grow in love, awe, and praise toward God. Every entry is a billboard advertising the grace and greatness of Jesus. Look to him. Worship your Savior with every ounce of your heart. Let's sing together as Christ's people, "Glory to the newborn King!"

Merry Christmas,
Jeff Medders

DAY 1

The Virgin Birth

Behold, the virgin shall conceive and bear a son…

ISAIAH 7:14

Let us go and stand by the manger to behold the commencement of the incarnation of Jesus. Let us recall the time when God first enveloped himself in mortal form and tabernacled among us. Let us not blush to go to so humble a spot; let us stand by that village inn, and let us see Jesus Christ, the God-man, become an infant of a span long.

And first, we see here, in speaking of this birth of Christ, a miraculous conception. The text says expressly, "Behold, the virgin shall conceive and bear a son." This expression is unparalleled even in sacred Scripture. Of no other woman could it be said, beside the virgin Mary, and of no other man than Jesus Christ could it be written that his mother was a virgin. Therefore, he was not born of man, but the Holy Spirit overshadowed the virgin Mary, and Christ stands as the only man, save one other, who came forth pure from his Maker's hands, who could ever say, *I am pure.* Unblemished, born of the virgin Mary, begotten of the Holy Spirit, without a taint of sin. His soul was pure and spotless as the driven snow—white, clear, perfect—and his life was the same. In him was no sin. He took our infirmities and bore our sorrows on the cross. He was in all points tempted as we are, but there was that sweet exception, "... yet without sin" (Hebrews 4:15). A lamb without blemish. You who have known the Lord—who have tasted of his grace, who have held fellowship with him—does your heart acknowledge that he is a lamb without blemish? Can you find any fault with your Savior? Has his truthfulness departed? Have his words been broken? Have his promises failed? Has he forgotten his engagements? And, in any respect, can you find in him any blemish? Never! He is the unblemished Lamb: the pure, the spotless, the immaculate, "The Lamb of God, who takes away the sin of the world" (John 1:29), and in him there is no sin.

Tradition tells us that his manger was cut in the solid rock. There he was laid, and the oxen likely enough came to feed from the same manger, the hay and the fodder of which were his only bed. Oh, wondrous stoop of condescension, that our blessed Jesus should be girded with humility and stoop so low! Let us take courage here. If Jesus Christ was born in a manger in a rock, why should he not come and live in our rocky hearts? If he was born in a stable, why should the stable of our souls not be made into a habitation for him? If he was born in poverty, may not the poor in spirit expect that he will be their friend?

Oh, marvelous sight! Let us stand and look at it. A child of a virgin—what a mixture! There is the finite and the infinite; there is the mortal and the immortal; the manhood and the Godhead; time married to eternity; God linked with a creature; the vast unbounded one—whom earth could not hold and the heavens cannot contain—lying in his mother's arms. He who fastened the pillars of the universe and riveted the nails of creation hanging on a mortal breast, depending on a creature for nourishment. Oh, marvelous birth! Oh, miraculous conception! We stand and gaze and admire. It is a miracle of miracles that the infinite should become an infant—that he who is pure spirit and fills all things should be wrapped in swaddling bands and cradled in a manger.

If any troubled soul will look believingly at God in human flesh, we must take heart of hope. If we look believingly, his comfort will come speedily. The birth of Jesus is the proof of the goodwill of God to humanity; I am unable to conceive of proof more sure. He would not have come here to be born among us—to live among us, suffer and to die for us—if he had been slow to pardon or unwilling to save. O despairing soul, does not Immanuel, God with us, make it hard to doubt the mercy of the Lord? Oh, that the Holy Spirit would convey to each one of my readers the light which shines from the star of incarnation! At this moment, may the people who walk in darkness see in the incarnate God a great light, and perceive in him the prophecy and assurance of all good things! Not long shall evil oppress the believer, for in Christ Jesus God is with us, and if God be for us, who can be against us?

REFLECT

What is your soul's response to the miracle of the virgin birth? How does the humility of Jesus' birth bring you comfort today?

PRAY

Thank you, Jesus, for lying in the manger so you could be laid on the cross for my sins. I praise you for taking on flesh so that you could take away my sinful flesh. My heart is moved and comforted by your incarnation, which is an invitation to come to you for life everlasting. I'm yours, Jesus. Amen.

DAY 2

A Bright Promise

I will put enmity between you and the woman, and between your offspring and her offspring; he shall bruise your head, and you shall bruise his heel.

GENESIS 3:15

This is the first gospel sermon that was ever delivered upon the surface of this earth. Is it not remarkable that this great gospel promise should have been delivered so soon after Adam and Eve's transgression? As an oak lies within an acorn, all the great truths which make up the gospel of Christ lie within this promise.

Observe here the grand mystery of the incarnation. The words of this prophecy can refer to none other than the baby born in Bethlehem of the blessed virgin. It was she who conceived and bore a son, and it is concerning her son that we sing, "For to us a child is born, to us a son is given; and the government shall be upon his shoulder, and his name shall be called Wonderful Counselor,

Mighty God, Everlasting Father, Prince of Peace" (Isaiah 9:6). On the memorable night at Bethlehem, when angels sang in heaven, the offspring of the woman appeared. And as soon as the old serpent—the devil—saw the light, he entered into the heart of Herod to try and slay the offspring, but the Father preserved Jesus, and allowed no one to lay hands on him.

And here in Genesis 3:15, the sufferings of Christ are clearly foretold: "You shall bruise his heel." Within the compass of those words, we find the whole story of our Lord's sorrows, from Bethlehem to Calvary. And in the words, "He shall bruise your head," there is the breaking of Satan's regal power, the clearing away of sin, the destruction of death by resurrection, the leading of captives out in the ascension, the victory of truth in the world through the descent of the Spirit, the binding of Satan, and lastly, the casting of the evil one and all his followers into the lake of fire.

Both the conflict and the conquest are in these few fruitful words of Genesis 3:15. They may not have been fully understood by those who first heard them, but to us they are now full of light. The text at first looks like a flint, hard and cold, but sparks fly from it plentifully, for hidden fires of infinite love and grace lie concealed within.

This is the mother of all promises; the offspring of the woman shall bruise the serpent's head. In that one single promise—that God himself would provide a deliverer by whom the tempter should be destroyed and all his craft foiled—I see written as clearly as with a sunbeam that

God meant to have mercy upon man. He would not have talked about the offspring of the woman bruising the serpent's head if he had not intended something comforting for you and for me. Though he did drive our first parents out of Eden, he did not drive them down to hell. Though he did banish them from paradise, he did not immediately consign them to the flames of his wrath—but there and then gave them a bright promise, which for many hundreds of years was the only one that cheered the thick darkness of the Fall. That fact alone should make you hope that there is forgiveness with God.

Do you look to Jesus, the offspring of the woman? Are you trusting in him to break the power of the enemy? Do you wish the power of sin to be broken in yourself? Do you desire to have the very head of it crushed to powder? Do you pine to be free from sin and holy as God is holy? Are you trusting in Jesus to have this same thing wrought in you? Ah, then you are on the conquering side! Victory shall be yours through the blood of the Lamb! Over this promise of a gracious God we ought to rejoice exceedingly! We have found much gospel in the wonderful sentence pronounced upon that old serpent, the devil, and yet we have only skimmed the surface.

REFLECT

How does Genesis 3:15 help you understand the entire Old Testament and the birth of Christ? Look at Spurgeon's questions in the paragraph above, and spend a few moments meditating on the one that gets your attention.

PRAY

Holy Father, thank you for your Son—the promised offspring of the woman, who would destroy the devil, death, and all my sin. Thank you, Jesus, for enduring suffering for my sake. Holy Spirit, help me to rejoice and live in the victory of Christ during this season and beyond. You are the God who keeps his promises! In the name of Jesus, every promise of yours is "Yes and amen." Amen.

DAY 3

To Destroy the Devil

The reason the Son of God appeared was to destroy the works of the devil.

1 JOHN 3:8

Ring out sweetly, all the silver bells of earth and all the golden harps of heaven, for God has purposed that every atom of the terrible work of the devil upon the earth shall be destroyed!

Christ's incarnation was a fatal blow to the works of Satan. Uprising from his divine retreat in eternity, he appeared in human form and thereby scattered and utterly destroyed the works of darkness. Did God come down to men? Was he incarnate in the infant that slept in Bethlehem's manger? If it be so, the Almighty has not then given up our nature to be the prey of sin. Do not despair! If one has been born on earth who is divine as well as human, then rejoice, O race of Adam! Recall the song, "Glory to God in the highest, and on earth peace among those with whom he is pleased!" (Luke 2:14). For the Lord Jesus will so break the head of the old dragon that he shall never wear the crown again.

It was in his death that Jesus chiefly overthrew Satan and destroyed his works. Marvel of marvels, the judge stands where the criminal should have stood and is "numbered with the transgressors" (Isaiah 53:12)! Behold, the wrath of God has fallen upon his well-beloved; Jesus has suffered that he may reconcile us to God and heal the breach which sin had caused. The deed was done. Jesus has, by his unutterable beauties, removed the deformities of all who are in him. By his obedience unto death, the law is vindicated, justice is honored, and grace is glorified.

It never entered Satan's thoughts that God himself could deign to suffer and to die. He did not know the boundless love and wisdom of Jehovah. Even his angelic intellect could never have conceived the matchless plan of atonement by a sacrifice: propitiation by substitution. The blessed fact of the Son of God becoming manifest in human flesh and dying in human form to destroy the works of the devil did not enter into a creature's mind. Yet this was always in God's purpose, for the better display of his divine attributes. Behind and under and over the works of the devil, the Lord had ever the design that this evil should be permitted that he might baffle it with love and that the glory of his grace might be revealed.

Mark that word "destroyed"—not limited nor alleviated nor neutralized but destroyed. O brothers and sisters, what could you and I do against such a power as Satan? Who among us can loosen his works and cast his cords from us? Being ourselves originally under Satan's power—being ourselves destroyed—could we destroy the destroyer? Could we, while yet enemies of God, tear out that enmity? No, another hand must make us friends—a hand outside of us. That which has been done by the powers of darkness must be undone by the eternal light, or else it will remain forever.

The Lord will never turn from his promise to bruise Satan under his feet and cast him into the lake of fire. There is a deadly, implacable, infinite, eternal hatred between Christ and that sin of which Satan is the representative. Sin is so abominable in the sight of God and of good men that its various forms are said to be "the works of the devil." Do not laugh at sin—do not dare to trifle with it; it is dangerous and deadly because it is of the devil, from whom no good thing can ever come. Oh, if we could but see the slime of the serpent upon our pleasurable sins, the venom of snakes upon our little lusts, and the smoke of hell upon our proud and boastful thoughts, surely we would loathe that which we should never delight in! May it enter into our hearts and make sin horrible to us.

Has the Son of God appeared to you to destroy the works of the devil in you? Is that enmity in your heart toward God destroyed? Has the love of God in Christ Jesus appeared to you in such a way that you can truly say you no longer hate God but love him? Has the Son of God destroyed all your self-righteousness? Have all those rags gone from you? Why, if we were to talk about our own righteousness, we should be fools and liars in one. We have no righteousness of our own—we dare not dream of such a thing. Is this your case? Then the Lord Jesus Christ has been manifested to destroy in you the works of the devil.

REFLECT

How does today's reading speak to the way you view sin? Are there any temptations or sins that need the demolishing grace of Christ? How are you benefiting from the full assurance of Christ's work?

PRAY

Lord Jesus, since you appeared on earth to destroy the works of the devil, keep me from aligning with the devil's agenda again. I don't want to toy with sin, minimize it or entertain temptations—may all my sins be grotesque in my eyes and heart. I need to be both repulsed and rejoicing! Your incarnation, crucifixion, and resurrection are my ammunition against the devil. Thank you for appearing on earth to set me free and destroy my enemy! I rejoice in my Redeemer! Amen.

DAY 4

Grace from Bethlehem

But you, O Bethlehem Ephrathah, who are too little to be among the clans of Judah, from you shall come forth for me one who is to be ruler in Israel, whose coming forth is from of old, from ancient days.

MICAH 5:2

The little village of Bethlehem was dear to every Israelite. Jerusalem might have outshone it in splendor, for it was "beautiful in elevation" (Psalm 48:2), and there stood the temple—the glory of the whole earth. Yet, around Bethlehem there clustered a number of incidents which always made it a pleasant resting-place to every Jewish mind. And we Christians cannot help loving Bethlehem.

It was at Bethlehem that Ruth went to glean in the fields of Boaz. It was there that Boaz looked upon her and she bowed herself before him. It was there that her marriage was celebrated, and in the streets of Bethlehem did Boaz and Ruth receive a blessing which made them fruitful, so that Boaz became the father of Obed, and Obed the father of Jesse, and Jesse the father of David. That last fact gilds Bethlehem with glory: the fact that David was born there—the mighty hero who smote the Philistine giant, who led the discontented of his land away from the tyranny of their monarch, and who afterwards, by the full consent of a willing people, was crowned king of Israel and Judah. Bethlehem was a royal city because the kings were brought forth from there. Little as Bethlehem was, it was much to be esteemed.

Next, there is something in the name—"Bethlehem" *Ephrathah*—which means "the house of bread." Ought not Jesus Christ to be born in "the house of bread?" He is the bread of his people, on which they feed. As our fathers ate manna in the wilderness, so do we live on Jesus here below. And in that blessed bread of heaven, made of the bruised body of our Lord Jesus and baked in the furnace of his agonies, we find a blessed food. There is no food like Jesus to the desponding soul or to the strongest saint.

Now consider that word *Ephrathah*. That was the old name of the place, which the Jews retained and loved. The meaning of it is "fruitfulness" or "abundance." Ah! Well, was Jesus born in the house of fruitfulness, for where does our fruitfulness come from but from Bethlehem? Our poor, barren hearts never produced one fruit or flower till they were watered with the Savior's blood. It is his incarnation which fattens the soil of our hearts. There had been thorns on all the ground and mortal poisons before he came, but our fruitfulness comes from him. "I am like an evergreen cypress; from me comes your fruit" (Hosea 14:8). And "All my springs are in you" (Psalm 87:7). If we be like trees planted by the rivers of water, bringing forth our fruit in our season, it is not because we are naturally fruitful but because of the rivers of water by which we were planted. It is Jesus that makes us fruitful. "Whoever abides in me," he says, "and I in him, he it is that bears much fruit" (John 15:5). Glorious Bethlehem Ephrathah! Rightly named! Fruitful house of bread—the house of abundant provision for the people of God!

Do you see the reason why he was sent by the Father? He came to be "ruler in Israel." There is emphatic meaning in that verse that we sing:

Born thy people to deliver;
Born a child, and yet a king.[1]

The moment he came to earth, he was a king. He did not wait till maturity to take his empire, but as soon as his eye greeted the sunshine, he was a king. From the moment his little hands grasped anything, they grasped a scepter. As soon as his pulse beat and his blood began to flow, his heart beat royally, and his pulse beat an imperial measure, and his blood flowed in a kingly current. He was born a king. He came "to be ruler in Israel."

Does he rule in your heart? Does he command your will? Do you ever seek counsel at his hand in your difficulties? Do you desire to honor him and to put crowns upon his head? Is he your ruler? Blessed Lord Jesus! You are the ruler of your people's hearts, and you ever shall be. We want no other ruler but you, and we will submit to none other. We are free because we are the servants of Christ. We are at liberty because he is our ruler, and we know no bondage and no slavery because Jesus Christ alone is monarch of our hearts.

REFLECT

How is your soul being filled and satisfied by Christ, the bread of Life born in the "house of bread"? What evidences of grace do you see that Christ is your ruler, the true monarch of your life?

PRAY

Jesus, only you could be the newborn King. Rule in my heart today, my King. Keep me from eyeing the kingdom of darkness and its tempting but enslaving tricks and traps. Let me hear the joyous music of your kingdom; draw me near to your gracious and glorious throne, where you satisfy my soul with joy in you. All glory be to you, my Lord, my Savior, my God. Amen.

DAY 5

The Fullness of Time

But when the fullness of time had come, God sent forth his Son, born of woman, born under the law, to redeem those who were under the law, so that we might receive adoption as sons.

GALATIANS 4:4–5

God had promised to our forefather Adam in the garden that a mysterious offspring of the woman should be born and should bruise the serpent's head. In mysterious signs, he had shown to his people that a Messiah was coming; by many of his prophets, he had spoken of Immanuel, "God with us" (Isaiah 7:14, see footnote). But for thousands of years the Lord did not come; though sin was rampant and the darkness dense, nothing could excite the Lord to an unwise haste. But the "fullness of time had come," and suddenly, amid the darkness of the night, there was heard sweeter singing than had ever come from mortal lips: "Glory to God in the highest, and on earth peace among those with whom he is pleased!" (Luke 2:14). What lit up the sky with unprecedented splendor, and what filled the air with chorales at the dead of night? See, there in Bethlehem's manger! That same one who had given the promise come down to earth to be a man and to give himself for us. Think of him, "when the fullness of time had come," descending from the throne of infinite majesty to the manger of humiliation and being there, as a babe, swaddled in his weakness. Will you not love him who became God incarnate for you?

I invite you to consider the joyful mission of the Son of God. The Lord of heaven has come to earth; God has taken upon himself human nature. Hallelujah! Observe that the Lord was moving towards man: "But when the fullness of time had come, *God* sent forth his Son." We did not move towards the Lord, but the Lord towards us. I do not find the world in repentance seeking after its Maker. No, the offended God himself, in infinite compassion, broke the silence and came forth to bless his enemies. All good things begin with him. For the birth of Jesus is the grandest light of history—the sun in the heavens of all time. It is the pole star of human destiny, the hinge of chronology, the meeting-place of the waters of the past and the future.

I hope it may not seem wearisome to you if I dwell upon that word "sent": "God *sent* forth his Son." I take great pleasure in that expression, for it seals the whole work of Jesus. Everything that Christ did was done by commission and authority of his Father. The great Lord, when he was born at Bethlehem and assumed our nature, did it under divine authorization. And admire how God has only one begotten Son and has sent him to uplift us. The messenger to man must be none other than God's own Son. What dignity is here! It is the Lord of angels that is born of Mary; it is he, without whom nothing was made, wrapped in swaddling bands. Oh, the dignity of this and, consequently, the efficiency of it! He who has come to save us is no weak creature like ourselves; he who has taken upon himself our nature is no being of limited strength—such as an angel or a seraph might have been—but he is the Son of the Highest. Glory be to his blessed name!

Let us dwell on this with delight and press on, keeping to the very words of the text, for they are very sweet. God sent his Son in real humanity, "born of woman." Christ was really and truly of the substance of his mother, as certainly as any other infant that is born into the world is so. God did not create the human nature of Christ apart and then transmit it into mortal existence by some special means; but his Son was made and born of a woman. I beg you to rejoice in this near approach of Christ to us. Ring out the glad bells, if not in the spires and steeples, yet within your own hearts. For gladder news has never greeted your ear than this: the Son of God was also "born of woman."

Still further, it is added, that God sent his Son "born under the law." And now admire and wonder! The Son of God has come under the law. He was the law-maker and the law-giver, and he is both the judge of the law and the executioner of the law, and yet he himself came under the law. He obeyed to the full both the first and the second tables of the Ten Commandments, for he loved God with all his heart and his neighbor as himself. As our surety and substitute, he came under the curse of the law, being made a curse for us (Galatians 3:13). Having taken our place and adopted our nature—though without sin himself—he came under the rigorous demands of justice, and in due time he bowed his head to the sentence of death. He died—the righteous for the unrighteous—to bring us to God (1 Peter 3:18). In heaven we shall probably discover that Christ came to die for our sins precisely at the only fitting moment—that in fact redemption's work could not have been so wisely accomplished at the gates of the Garden of Eden as on Calvary and that the reign of Herod and the Roman Caesar afforded the most fitting era for the sacrifice of the cross.

I do not wonder why people of the world celebrate the supposed anniversary of the great birthday as a high festival with carols and banquets. While knowing nothing of the spiritual meaning of the mystery, they perceive that it means humanity's good, and so, in their own way, they respond to it. But to those who are truly the people of God, the incarnation is the object of a thoughtful joy. The birth of our Lord Jesus Christ into this world is a wellspring of pure, unmingled joy. The angelic song was a fit accompaniment to the joyful event. We may sing with undivided joy, "For to us a child is born, to us a son is given" (Isaiah 9:6).

REFLECT

Why is it vital that our Savior was born "of woman" and "under the law"? How does the providence and plan of God in the birth of Christ move you to worship and thanksgiving this Christmas?

PRAY

Holy Father, how sweet it is to hear about this "fullness of time"—that the Son was sent for me according to your sovereign grace. Your gracious plan of redemption is the great cause of my praise, my joy, my all. If you had not moved toward me in mercy and love, I would continue wallowing in the darkness. But thanks to you, I have seen the great light, and I believe in the Son, my Savior, Jesus Christ, in whose name I celebrate in this season and every season. Amen.

DAY 6

Sending His Own Son

For God has done what the law, weakened by the flesh, could not do. By sending his own Son in the likeness of sinful flesh and for sin, he condemned sin in the flesh.

ROMANS 8:3

The law of God is perfect. You cannot add anything to it, nor take anything from it, without spoiling it. But there are some things which the law cannot do.

It cannot produce a new heart in a sinner. It cannot save a lost soul. It cannot justify a guilty person. It cannot draw a wanderer back to God. The law tells us what we ought to do, but that does not enable us to do it. And though it reveals our sin, our shortcomings, and our transgressions, it cannot remove the sin or the transgression from us. It is weak for that purpose because it was never intended to accomplish such an end.

Hear these words of God: "by sending"! From yonder throne, beyond your sight, and higher than your loftiest imagination, he sends. And who does God send? An angel? An archangel? No! In the fullness of time, God sent, as he is called in the text, "his own Son." Jesus Christ, the Son of God, was born into this world, and he took upon himself our humanity. The Word was made flesh and dwelt among us, and the apostles declare that they beheld his glory—the glory of the only begotten of the Father, full of grace and truth. The text uses very important words. It says that God sent his Son "in the likeness of sinful flesh"—not in the likeness of flesh, for that would not be true, but in the same likeness as our sinful flesh. He was, to all intents and purposes, like ourselves: tempted in all points as we are, though without sin, with all our sinless infirmities and with all our tendencies to suffer. He was perfectly human, and God sent him in the likeness of sinful flesh.

Though it is 2,000 years ago and more, the Christmas bells seem to ring on. The joy of his coming is still in our hearts. He lived here for his 32 or 33 years, but he was sent, the text tells us, for a reason which caused him to die. He was sent "for sin." This may mean that he was sent to do battle with sin or that he was sent because sin was in the world—or, best of all, that he was sent to be a sin-offering. He was sent that he might be the substitute for sinners. God's great plan was this: that since his justice could not overlook sin and sin must be punished, Jesus Christ should come and take the sin of his people upon himself, and upon the accursed tree—the cross of wretched note—should suffer what was due on our behalf. And that then, through his sufferings, the infinite love of

God should stream forth without any violation of his infinite justice. This is what God did. He sent his Son to Bethlehem; he sent his Son to Calvary; he sent his Son down to the grave; and he has now recalled him unto the excellent glory where he sits at the right hand of God. The incarnation of Christ is a great reality which we can never understand but which we devoutly believe. And believing it, we have before us God's way of doing what the law could not do.

The wounds of Jesus can do what nothing else can do. When I am pardoned, I hate sin, and when I see the love of God in Christ Jesus, sin becomes a condemned and destroyed thing. If Jesus paid the debt, it is paid, and I am clear. "There is therefore now no condemnation for those who are in Christ Jesus" (Romans 8:1). Your only question, dear readers, is this: was Christ sent for you; did he suffer for you; was he a substitute for you? According to this grand old book on which we fix our trust as an infallible guide in this matter, Jesus died for every soul that trusts him. So it is written, "Whoever believes and is baptized will be saved" (Mark 16:16). Do you have these personal evidences? Do you truly trust him? Then you are forgiven. You are this day absolved. You may rejoice in God through our Lord Jesus Christ, by whom you have now received the atonement. Your sins—past, present, and future—are all blotted out. He was sent for this, for you.

REFLECT

How does the Father sending the Son comfort your soul today? What would change in your life if you tasted more fully of the sweetest thought: that Christ was sent to remove your sin?

PRAY

Holy Father, let me hear the Christmas bells loud and clear today. The gospel is just as fresh today, losing no sweetness 2,000 years later. Electrify my heart with the glorious news that Christ has done what the law could never do for me and what I could never do for myself. I am new; I am saved; I am free! Hallelujah! Thank you, Jesus! Amen.

DAY 7

He Will Be Great

He will be great and will be called
the Son of the Most High.

LUKE 1:32

Fine words would be but tawdry things to hang beside the unspeakably glorious Lord. Jesus is such a one that no eloquence can ever reach the height of his glory, and the simplest words are best suited to a subject so sublime. I can say no more than that he is great. If I could tell forth his greatness with choral symphonies of cherubim, I should still fail to reach the height of this great argument. I will be content if I can touch the hem of the garment of his greatness. We shall not labor, therefore, to preserve the niceties of theology, but we shall freely speak of our Lord in his Godhead and in his manhood, and apply our text to the whole Christ, declaring the divine promise that "He will be great."

Let me touch this theme as best I can by saying of our adorable Lord Jesus that he is great from many points of view. I might have said from every point of view, but that is too large a truth to be surveyed at one sitting. Mind would fail us, life would fail us, and time would fail us: eternity and perfection will alone suffice for that boundless meditation. But from the points of view to which I would conduct you for a moment, the Lord Jesus Christ is emphatically great.

First, Jesus Christ is great in the perfection of his nature. Think, my brothers and sisters, there was never such a being as our well-beloved. He is peerless and incomparable. He is divine and therefore unique. He is "Light of light, very God of very God."[2] Jesus is truly equal with God, one with the Father. Oh, the greatness of Godhead! Jehovah is a being infinite, immeasurable, incomprehensible, inconceivable! He fills all things and yet is not contained by all things. He is indeed great beyond any idea of greatness that has ever dawned upon us. All this is true of the only-begotten.

But our Lord Jesus is also man, and this makes the singularity of his person: that he should be perfectly and purely God and, as truly and really, man. He is not humanity deified; he is not Godhead humanized. He is God. He is man. He is all that God is and all that man is as God created him. He is as truly God as if he were not man and yet as completely and perfectly man as if he were not God. Think of this wondrous combination! A perfect human without spot or stain of original or actual sin, and then the glorious Godhead combined with it! Am I not right in saying that Jesus stands alone? He is one with us and yet inconceivably beyond us. Our nature is limited, sinful, fallen; but his nature is unbounded, holy, divine.

He is also great in the grandeur of his offices. Remember that he has for our sakes undertaken to be our Redeemer. You see your bondage, brothers and sisters. You know it, for some of you have worn the chains till they have entered into your soul, and from such slavery he came to redeem us. He comes to rebuild and to restore. To accomplish this, he came to be our Priest, our Prophet, and our King; in each office, he is glorious beyond compare. He came to be our Savior, our Sacrifice, our Substitute, our Surety, our Head, our Friend, our Lord, our Life, our All. Mention these offices as you can, and truly you shall never remember them all; for he, the express image of his Father's glory, has undertaken every kind of office, that he might perfectly redeem his people, and make them to be his own forever.

His nature and his offices would alone furnish us with a lengthened theme; but oh, my brothers and sisters, the Lord Jesus is great in the splendor of his achievements. His people's sins were laid upon him, and he bore them up to the cross, and on the cross he made an end of them, so that they will never be mentioned against his people anymore forever. Then he went down into the grave and slept there for a little season; but he tore away the bars of the grave and left death dead at his feet, bringing life and immortality to light by his resurrection. This was his high calling, and he has fulfilled it. Is it not proven that he is great? Conquerors are great, and he is the greatest of them. Deliverers are great, and he is the greatest of them. Liberators are great, and he is the greatest of them. Saviors are great, and he is the greatest of them. They that multiply the joys of men are truly great, and what shall I say of him who has bestowed everlasting joy upon his people? Well did you say, O Gabriel, "He will be great," for great indeed he is!

REFLECT

Which angle of Christ's greatness that Spurgeon has expounded stirs your heart? How is Christ's person and work igniting your praise?

PRAY

Pray to your Lord, listing the ways he is great, saying, "Lord, you are great because…"

DAY 8

Immeasurable Love

For God so loved the world, that he gave his only Son, that whoever believes in him should not perish but have eternal life. For God did not send his Son into the world to condemn the world, but in order that the world might be saved through him.

JOHN 3:16–17

Those who love much will give much, and you may usually measure the truth of love by its self-denials and sacrifices. That love which spares nothing, but spends itself to help and bless its object, is love indeed, and not the mere name of it.

Consider, then, what this gift was that God gave. I should have to labor for expression if I were to attempt to set forth fully this priceless boon, and I will not court a failure by attempting the impossible. I will only invite you to think of the sacred person whom the great Father gave in order that he might prove his love to humanity. It was his only begotten Son—his beloved Son—in whom he was well pleased. None of us ever had such a son to give. Ours are the sons of men; his was the Son of God. The Father gave his other self, one with himself. When the great God gave his Son, he gave God himself, for Jesus is not in his eternal nature less than God. What more could he give? God gave his all: he gave himself. Who can measure this love?

The great God has given his own Son, that "whoever believes in him should not perish." Trust in Christ is the certain way to eternal happiness. Now, what is it to believe in Jesus? It is, first, to give your firm and cordial assent to the truth that God did send his Son, born of a woman, to stand in the stead of guilty sinners. And that God put on him the iniquities of us all, so that he bore the punishment due to our transgressions—being made a curse for us. The first and immediate object of a sinner's justifying faith is God the Son, incarnate in human flesh and offering atonement for sinners.

Do you have the eye of faith? Then look to Christ as God. Bow before him and accept him as being "very God of very God," for if you do not, you have no part in him. Believe in him as fully human; believe the wondrous story of his incarnation. Rely upon the testimony of the evangelists, who declare that the infinite was robed in the infant, that the eternal was concealed within the mortal; that he who was King of heaven became a servant of servants and the Son of man. Believe and admire the mystery of his incarnation, for unless you believe this, you cannot be saved. View the

Lamb of God as silent before his shearers; view him as the man of sorrows and acquainted with grief. Go with him to Gethsemane and behold him sweating drops of blood. Be sure of this—your faith has nothing to do with anything within you.

Believe on him, then, who, on yonder tree with nailed hands and feet, pours out his life for sinners. There is the object of your faith for justification! Not yourself, nor anything which the Holy Spirit has done in you or anything he has promised to do for you, but look to Christ and to Christ Jesus alone. Then let your faith behold Christ as rising from the dead. He dies to pay the debt, and he rises that he may nail the handwriting of that discharged debt to the cross. See him ascending on high, and behold him this day pleading before the Father's throne. He is there pleading for his people, offering up today his authoritative petition for all who come to God by him. And he—as God, as man, as living, as dying, as rising, and as reigning above—he and he alone is to be the object of your faith for the pardon of sin. The essence of faith is trust, reliance, and dependence wholly on Christ. Fling away every other confidence of every sort, except confidence in Jesus. Do not allow a shade of a shadow of a confidence in anything that you can do or in anything that you can be, but look alone to him whom God has sent and set forth to be the propitiation for sin.

See, then, the love of God: that he gave his Son from of old and has never revoked the gift. He continues to give his dear Son to all who are willing to accept him. Out of the riches of his grace, he *has* given, is giving, and *will* give the Lord Jesus Christ, and all the priceless gifts which are contained in him, to all needy sinners who will simply trust him. In the gift of his only begotten Son, God commended his love to us, in that while we were yet sinners, in due time Christ died for the ungodly. The black background of sin makes the bright line of love shine out the more clearly. When the lightning writes the name of the Lord with flaming finger across the cloud of the storm, we are compelled to see it. So, when love inscribes the cross upon the jet tablet of our sin, even blind eyes must see that "in this is love" (1 John 4:10).

REFLECT

Is there anything you need to "fling away" so you can focus your faith and confidence on Christ alone? How are you resting and rejoicing in the incarnate, crucified, raised, and ascended Christ?

PRAY

Holy Father, during this Christmas season, and throughout the rest of my life, don't let me become numb to John 3:16. This famous text deserves more than a familiar agreement and assent to its truth. It warrants a heart set aflame by your love, a soul seized and set aright by your promise of eternal life in Christ. Stoke the flames today, my Lord and my God. In Christ's name, amen.

DAY 9

Call His Name Jesus

But as he considered these things, behold, an angel of the Lord appeared to him in a dream, saying, "Joseph, son of David, do not fear to take Mary as your wife, for that which is conceived in her is from the Holy Spirit. She will bear a son, and you shall call his name Jesus, for he will save his people from their sins."

MATTHEW 1:20-21

Nothing is more prominent about a person than their name. We can hardly mention someone without pronouncing their name, and so we cannot mention our Lord without speaking of salvation.

Our thoughts turn today to the first use of the name in connection with our Lord, when the child who was yet to be born was named Jesus. Here we find everything suggestive of comfort. The name of Jesus was sweet from the beginning because of the words with which it was accompanied, for they were meant to remove perplexity from Joseph's mind: "Do not fear." Truly, no name can banish fear like the name of Jesus; it is the beginning of hope and the end of despair. This name is full of rare delights when we meditate upon the infinite preciousness of the person to whom it was assigned.

According to the text, the angel brought a message from the Lord and said, "You shall call his name Jesus." It is a name which, like him who bears it, has come down from heaven. Our Lord has other names of office and relationship, but this is specially and peculiarly his own personal name, and it is the Father who has named him. JESUS is the most appropriate name that our Lord could receive. The name is the highest, brightest, and noblest of names; it is the glory of our Lord to be a Savior. It is a name which the Holy Spirit explains through the angel, as he tells us the reason for the name of Jesus: "For he will save his people from their sins." It is a name given to our Lord because "he saves"—not according to any temporary and common salvation, from enemies and troubles, but he saves from spiritual enemies and especially from sins. This is how Christ saves his people from their sin: by rescuing them, by the force of his love, out of the power, tyranny, and dominion of sins. Christ's shoulders bore the guilt of his people. He saves his people through his personal substitution on the cross, by standing in their stead and suffering in their place.

There is no other way of salvation but by his vicarious sufferings and death. This is the power which drives out the vipers of sin from the soul—the precious blood of Jesus. To the best that was ever born of woman, God has given the best name that any son of man could bear. His name is not Jesus because he is our example—though indeed he is perfection itself, and we long to tread in his footsteps—but his name is Jesus because he has come to save that which is lost. He is nothing if he is not the Savior.

Let us be glad that we have such a Savior, and that the name of Jesus retains all the sweetness and power it ever had and shall retain it till all the chosen people are saved, and then forever and ever. If he was Jesus in the cradle, what is he now that he is exalted in the heavens? As Immanuel, God with us, his very incarnation made him Jesus, the Savior of men—but what shall I say of him now that beyond his incarnation we have his atonement, and above his atonement his resurrection, and beyond that his ascension, and, to crown all, his perpetual intercession?

How grandly does the title befit him now that he is able to save to the uttermost those that come to God by him, seeing that he lives to make intercession for them! If in the arms of the virgin he is the Savior, what is he on the throne of God? If wrapped in swaddling bands he is Jesus, what is he now that the heavens have received him? If in the workshop of Nazareth and sitting in the temple among the doctors of religion, he was the child Jesus, the Savior, what is he now that his infancy and childhood are over and he is exalted far above all principalities and powers? If he was Jesus when on the cross, presenting himself as an offering for his people, what is he now that he has by one sacrifice perfected forever those that are set apart? What is he now that he sits at the right hand of God, waiting in expectation till his enemies are made his footstool? Let us all unite in calling our Lord by this tender human name of Jesus.

This name is Christ's *personal name* forever. It is the name his father gave him; it is the name his mother gave him—the child Jesus. We also belong to his family; for the one who believes in him is his father and mother and sister and brother, and that most dear and familiar name by which he was known at home is ever in our mouths. He is the Lord, and we worship him, and he is Jesus, and we love him.

Jesus is also his *heart name* and is full of the music of love. It is the name which moves our affections and fires our souls. Let your hearts go out towards him in tender union. Jesus is his *death name*—Jesus of Nazareth, King of the Jews, was written on his cross. That is his *resurrection name*. That is his *gospel name*, which we preach. It is the name which Peter preached to the Gentiles when he said, "Everyone who believes in him receives forgiveness of sins through his name" (Acts 10:43). And this, friends, is his *heaven name*. They sing to him there as Jesus. See how it concludes the Bible. Read Revelation, and read its songs, and see how they worship Jesus, the Lamb of God. Let us go and tell of this name! Let us continually meditate upon it. Let us love his name now and forever.

REFLECT

What stirs in your soul as you think of the name Jesus? Is it sweet to you to know his personal name? How does his name continually preach the gospel to you?

PRAY

Jesus, what a grace it is to know your name—my Friend, my Brother. What a mercy to believe in your name—my Savior, my Lord, my God. What power to say your name in prayer—my Help, my Rock, my Shepherd. Since your name will always be Jesus, my future will always be with you—saved and secure. In your name, Jesus, amen.

DAY 10

His Name Is Wonderful

For to us a child is born, to us a son is given; and the government shall be upon his shoulder, and his name shall be called Wonderful Counselor, Mighty God, Everlasting Father, Prince of Peace.

ISAIAH 9:6

Beloved, there are a thousand things in this world that are called by names that do not belong to them; but in entering upon my text, I must announce at the very opening that Christ is called Wonderful because he is so. God the Father never gave his Son a name which he did not deserve. There is no empty tribute here, no flattery. It is just the simple name that he deserves. Those who know him best will say that the word "Wonderful" does not overstrain his merits but rather falls infinitely short of his glorious deserving.

Gather up your thoughts, my readers, for a moment, and center them all on Christ, and you will soon see how wonderful he is. Consider his eternal existence:

"begotten of his Father from before all worlds"—being of the same substance with his Father, begotten, not made, coequal, coeternal, in every attribute "very God of very God."[3] Of course, the Godhead could not be born of woman. That was from everlasting and is to everlasting. Consider, again, the incarnation of Christ, and you will rightly say that his name deserves to be "Wonderful." Oh, world of wonders! What's that I see? The eternal of ages, whose hair is white like wool—as white as snow—becomes an infant. Can it be? Oh, wonder of wonders! Manger of Bethlehem, you have miracles poured into you. This is a sight that surpasses all others. We can talk of the sun, moon, and stars and consider the heavens—the work of God's fingers that he has ordained—but all the wonders of the universe shrink into nothing when we come to the mystery of the incarnation of the Lord Jesus Christ.

Let this truth sink into your souls: it was no inferior being who came from heaven "for your sake" (2 Corinthians 8:9), but it was very God of very God who loved you with an everlasting and infinite affection. I have often turned that thought over in my mind, but I have never been able to express it as I have wished. If I were told that all the sons of men cared for me, that would be but a drop in a bucket compared with Jehovah himself regarding me. If it were said that all the princes of the earth had fallen at some poor man's feet, and laid aside their dignities that they might relieve his necessities, it would be counted condescending kindness—but such an act would not be worthy to be spoken of in comparison with that infinite condescension and unparalleled love which brought the Savior from the skies to rescue and redeem such worthless rebels as we were. Look at the cross. See your Master. There he hangs. Lift his hands! They drop motionless by his side. His foot exhibits still the nail-print, but there is no mark of life. Perhaps this is the greatest wonder of all: that he who is "death of death and hell's destruction"4 should for a while endure the bonds of death. But here is the wonder. He could not be held to those bonds. Oh! The risen Savior—you who could not see corruption—you are wonderful in your resurrection. And you are wonderful in your ascension!

What a list of glories we have here! What a burst of song it makes when we sing of the Messiah: "And his name shall be called Wonderful Counselor, Mighty God, Everlasting Father, Prince of Peace"! It is all very well to hear players on instruments and sweet singers rehearse these words, but to believe them and realize them in your own soul is better far. When every fear and every hope and every power and every passion of our nature fills the orchestra of our heart and all unite in one inward song unto the glorious Immanuel, what music it is! Get Christ Jesus in your soul, as the incarnate God, and he will set up a government within your nature which shall bring you peace, righteousness, joy, and eternal glory. He will so reign over you that your happiness shall know no bounds. You shall climb from grace to grace, from joy to joy, from peace to peace, yes, from heaven to the highest heaven. This all along shall be your divinest comfort: that Jesus is both God and man—even God with us.

There are no mysteries equal to this mystery; there is no surprise equal to this surprise; there is no astonishment, no admiration, that should equal the astonishment and admiration that we feel when we behold Christ. He surpasses everything. Christ deserves to be called Wonderful, not only because he is always wonderful and because he is surpassingly wonderful but also because he is altogether wonderful. If you look at Christ anyhow, anywhere, anyway, he is altogether wonderful: always to be looked at and always to be admired as wonderful.

REFLECT

What is it about Christ's character, offices, person, work, and words that you find to be exceedingly wonderful?

PRAY

Jesus, your name is Wonderful. Your incarnation, divinity, humanity, humility—all that you are and all that you do—is wonderful. Wonderful Christ, you are far from being dull, uninteresting, or mundane. Thrill me again this Christmas with the wonder of wonders—God is with us, God is for us, and God loves us. In the name of Jesus the Wonderful, amen.

DAY 11

His Name Is Immanuel

"Behold, the virgin shall conceive and bear a son, and they shall call his name Immanuel" (which means, God with us).

MATTHEW 1:23

Those words—"which means"—salute my ear with much sweetness. Why should the word "Immanuel" in Hebrew be interpreted at all? Was it not to show that it has reference to us Gentiles, and therefore it needed to be interpreted into one of the chief languages of the then-existing Gentile world: namely, Greek? This "which means" at Christ's birth and the three languages employed in the inscription upon the cross at his death show that he is not the Savior of the Jews only but also of the Gentiles. It must mean that different nations are addressed. We have the text put first in the Hebrew—"Immanuel"—and afterwards it is translated into the Gentile tongue—"God with us"—"which means" that we may know that we are invited, that we are welcome, that

God has seen our needs and has provided for us, and that now we may freely come: even we who were Gentile sinners and far off from God.

I do not expect in this meditation to be able to set forth all the meaning of this short text, "God with us," for indeed, it seems to me to contain the whole history of redemption. You may divide the text into two portions: "*God*," and then "God *with us*." We must dwell with equal emphasis upon each portion. The very essence and glory of the incarnation is that he was God, who was veiled in human flesh. If it were any other being who came to us in human flesh, I see nothing very remarkable in it—nothing comforting. That an angel should become a man is a matter of no great consequence to me; that some other superior being should assume the nature of man brings no joy to my heart and opens no well of consolation to me. But "God with us" is exquisite delight.

All that "God" means—the Deity, the infinite Jehovah with us—is worthy of the burst of midnight song, when angels startled the shepherds with their carols, singing, "Glory to God in the highest, and on earth peace among those with whom he is pleased!" (Luke 2:14). He who was born at Bethlehem is God and "God with us." *God*—there lies the majesty; "God *with us*"—there lies the mercy. *God*—therein is glory; "God *with us*"—therein is grace. "God" alone might well strike us with terror, but "God with us" inspires us with hope and confidence. Take my text as a whole and carry it in your hearts as a bundle of sweet spices to perfume your hearts with peace and joy.

This glorious word "Immanuel" means, first, that God in Christ is with us in very near association. It is not merely "in company with us," as another Greek word would signify, but "with," "together with," and "sharing with." This preposition is a metal rivet, a firm bond, implying—if not declaring—close fellowship. Now, think for a while, and you will see that God has truly come near to us in very close association. He must have done so, for he has taken upon himself our nature—literally our nature. Flesh, blood, bone—everything that makes a body. Mind, heart, soul, memory, imagination, judgment—everything that makes a rational man. Being with us in our nature, God was with us in the pilgrimage of life. Were you in the cradle? He was there. Were you a child under parental authority? Christ was also a boy in the home at Nazareth. Are you alone? So was he, in the wilderness and on the mountainside and in the garden's gloom. Do you labor in public society? So did he labor.

Next, take hold of the sweetness in his being "God with us" in our sorrows. There is no pain that breaks our hearts or disturbs our bodies that is foreign to Jesus Christ. Do you endure the grief of bereavement? Jesus "wept" at the tomb of Lazarus (John 11:35). Have you been slandered for righteousness' sake, and has it vexed your spirit? He could say, "Reproaches have broken my heart" (Psalm 69:20). Have you been betrayed? Do not forget that he had a familiar friend who sold him for the price of a slave. On what stormy seas have you been tossed which have not also roared around his boat? In the fires and in the rivers, in the cold night and under the burning sun, when you stoop down you will discover the footprints of the crucified one and hear him cry, "Fear not, for I am with you; be not dismayed, for I am your God" (Isaiah 41:10).

Do not be afraid to come to the gentle Jesus. Anyone could have come to the babe in Bethlehem. The oxen ate of the hay on which he slept and feared not. Jesus is the Friend of each one of us, even though we are sinful and unworthy. Do not stay back through fear of your unfitness; the shepherds came to him in all their disheveled state. Come, and welcome, for God indeed is "God with us."

REFLECT

Meditate on the Bible's intentional translation of "Immanuel." What gospel encouragements do you find? In what parts and places in your life do you need to believe God is with you?

PRAY

Lord, the sweetness of "Immanuel" is a deep delight. Widen and expand the capacity of my heart and mind to make full use and full enjoyment of "God with us." Tender comforts, soul-strengthening hope, and gospel assurance are found *in* you, *with* you, and *from* you, my Immanuel. Enable me to see and believe that right now, tomorrow, and in any and every condition of life, you are with me. In a sense, Christmas never ends. In the name of Jesus, my Savior, amen.

DAY 12

Christ Our Righteousness

And this is the name by which he will be called: "The Lord *is our righteousness."*

JEREMIAH 23:6

I find that many Christians who are very clear about being saved by the merits of Christ's death do not seem to understand the merits of his life.

Remember, believers, that from the first moment when Christ lay in the cradle until the time when he ascended on high, he was at work for his people. From the moment when he was seen in Mary's arms till the instant when, in the arms of death, he "bowed his head and gave up his spirit" (John 19:30), he was at work for your salvation and mine. He completed the work of obedience in his life and said to his Father, "I glorified you on earth, having accomplished the work that you gave me to do" (John 17:4). Then he completed the work of atonement in his death, and knowing that all things were accomplished, he cried, "It is finished"

(John 19:30). Through his life, he was spinning the thread to make the royal garment, and in his death, he dipped that garment in his blood. You have as much to thank Christ for living as for dying, and you should be as reverently and devoutly grateful for his spotless life as for his terrible death.

The text speaking of Christ, the son of David, the branch out of the root of Jesse, styles him, "The LORD ... our righteousness." The pith, however, of the title, lies in the little word "our." This is the grappling iron with which we get a hold on him—this is the anchor which dives into the bottom of this great deep of his immaculate righteousness. This is the sacred rivet by which our souls are joined to him. This is the blessed hand with which our soul touches him, and he becomes to us all in all: "The LORD ... *our* righteousness."

Let us observe a most precious doctrine—the imputed righteousness of Christ, unfolded in this title of our Lord and Savior. When we believe in Christ, by faith we receive our justification. As the merit of his blood takes away our sin, so the merit of his obedience is imputed to us for righteousness. As soon as we believe, God looks upon us as though that perfect obedience of Christ had been performed by us. God considers us as though we were Christ—looks upon us as though his life had been our life—and accepts, blesses, and rewards us as though all that he did had been done by us, his believing people. We must believe that the righteousness in which we must be clothed, and through which we must be accepted, and by which we are made to inherit eternal life can be no other than the work of Jesus Christ. We believe that the life of Christ constitutes the righteousness in which his people are to be clothed. His death washed away our sins; his life covered us from head to foot. His death was the sacrifice to God; his life was the gift to mankind by which a person satisfies the demands of the law. Here, the law is honored, and the soul is accepted.

Brothers and sisters, the Law-Giver has himself obeyed the law. Don't you think his obedience will be sufficient? Jehovah, the Lord himself, became human so that he may do our work—do you think he has done it imperfectly? Jehovah—he who girds the angels that excel in strength—has taken upon himself the form of a servant that he may become obedient. Do you think his service will be incomplete? Let the fact that the Savior is Jehovah strengthen your confidence. Be bold. Be very courageous. Face heaven and earth and hell with the challenge of the apostle: "Who shall bring any charge against God's elect?" (Romans 8:33). Look back upon your past sins, look upon your present infirmities and all your future errors, and, while you weep the tears of repentance, let no fear of damnation blanch your cheek. Does yesterday's sin make you stammer? In the teeth of all your sins, believe that he is your righteousness still. Your good works do not improve his righteousness; your bad works do not sully it. This is a robe which your best deeds cannot mend and your worst deeds cannot mar. You stand in him, not in yourself. Whatever, then, your doubts and fears may have been, poor troubled, distressed, distracted believer, do now say again, "Yes, he is the Lord my righteousness."

Every believer is as clean in the sight of God as the snow which falls from heaven. Come, then, let us shake off these fears. He who knows that his debt is paid would be foolish to be troubled about the debt, and she who knows her sin is forgiven may have, should have, ought to have peace with God through Jesus Christ his Lord. My dear brothers and sisters, God will help us to live more and more in the atmosphere of peace with God. I do believe the devil often worries us when there is no cause whatever for our being troubled. Sin is always to be hateful to us—we are always to loathe it; but, when washed in the precious blood of Jesus, we are to endeavor to realize that through his blood we are clean and that, with his spotless garments on, we are holy as the Holy One.

Notwithstanding the depravity of our old nature and the workings of the flesh against which we strive, we are accepted in the Beloved. We are justified by faith which is in Christ Jesus. Come, then, children of God: take your harps down from the willows and tune them to a rapturous strain. Magnify the Lord your righteousness. This is the name he shall be called: the Lord our righteousness—"Jehovah Tsidkenu." His name shall be rapturous on our lips and glorious in our ears, from this time forth, forever and ever. He appeared in his world to put away sin, and it is put away; let us, then, enjoy our rest.

REFLECT

What aspects and angles of Christ being your righteousness are especially precious to you today? What plagues your enjoyment of being declared righteous in Christ?

PRAY

O Lord, you alone are my righteousness. Your righteous life—from womb to tomb to throne—is all my hope and confidence in the Christian life. Help me enjoy the gospel reality of being called and counted righteous in you. Christmas is the reminder that you came to be my righteousness. The devil and my flesh will lie and try to get me doubting my share in "The Lord *our* righteousness." But I trust and treasure your name. You are *my* righteousness, Jesus. Amen.

DAY 13

Full of Grace and Truth

And the Word became flesh and dwelt among us,
and we have seen his glory, glory as of the only
Son from the Father, full of grace and truth.

JOHN 1:14

I get a great deal of comfort out of many doctrines, but the bottom comfort of my soul is this fact: that he who made the heavens and the earth, and without whom was not anything made that was made, was born of the virgin Mary at Bethlehem, and for 30 years and more did actually—not in fiction or myth but in very deed—dwell as a man among humanity. That fact is my soul's food. The historical fact that Christ Jesus was flesh and blood, bone of our bone, flesh of our flesh, a man like ourselves—this, I say, is nourishment to our spirits, and, believing it, we feel a joy unutterable, for we know that he who sits upon the throne of God is a man. It is the greatest miracle that was ever heard or read of: that "the Word became flesh and dwelt among us." To you and to me, the marvel is in the motive which prompted the incarnation.

What could it have been that brought Immanuel to such a stoop as this? What unrivaled, indescribable, unutterable love was this that made him leave his Father's glory, the adoration of angels, and all the hallowed joy of heaven, that he might be made a man like ourselves, to suffer, to bleed, to die? A prince who puts aside his crown and clothes himself with beggar's rags to investigate the miseries of his country is but a worm condescending to his fellow worms. But here is the Creator taking the creature into union with himself, the immortal becoming mortal, the omnipotent taking weakness—even human weakness—into union with his own person. We have perceived that he is bone of our bone and flesh of our flesh: man in all weaknesses of man but not man in any guiltiness of his own. Weak, suffering, hungry, thirsty, dying; but without spot or wrinkle, pure, the immaculate Lamb of God. Not God deteriorated to man, nor man deified to God, but God. God in all that is God-like, man in all that is manlike; and we have adored him as such. Indeed, so marvelous it is that, while we do find in the pagan mythologies instances of the gods appearing in the likeness of men, yet never do we see anything like the hypostatic union of the two natures in the person of Christ. Human wisdom in its most happy moments has never risen to anything like the thought of deity taking on manhood that humanity might be redeemed. Oh, the depth of the love of Jesus! Behold his glory!

I like to think of the wording of our text: that Christ is "full of grace and truth." This grace and truth are blended. The "and" between the two words I would treat as more than a common conjunction. The two rivers unite in one fullness—"full of grace and truth"; that is to say, the grace is truthful grace. Grace not in fiction nor in fancy, grace not to be hoped for and to be dreamed of, but grace of which every atom is fact; redemption which does redeem, pardon which does blot out sin, renewal which actually regenerates and salvation which completely saves. We have not here blessings which charm the ear and cheat the soul but real, substantial grace from God, which cannot lie. Now blend these things the other way: the Lord has come to bring us truth, but it is not the kind of truth which censures, condemns, and punishes. It is gracious truth: truth steeped in love—truth saturated with mercy. The truth which Jesus brings to his people comes not from the judgment seat but from the mercy seat. There is grace to God's people in everything that falls from the lips of Jesus Christ. See how grace and truth thus blend and qualify each other! The grace is all true, and the truth is all gracious. This is a wondrous compound made according to the art of the divine apothecary. Where else is grace so true or truth so gracious?

Brothers and sisters, since God in Christ is in the midst of us, let us abide in joyful, peaceful confidence in him who is grace and truth to us. Do not let us wander to other sources. To whom should we go? Shall we leave our God? Shall we leave his grace? Or his truth? Do not let us dream that he is changed, for he is God. Do not let us conceive that his grace and truth are exhausted, for his fullness is eternal. Let us receive strong comfort and remain steadfast—unmovable. Let us quietly rest in the firm belief that all we can want between here and heaven—all that we need in this moment and in all moments yet to come—is treasured up in Christ Jesus.

REFLECT

In what way does the fact of the incarnation nourish your soul? How does Christ being full of grace and truth comfort you?

PRAY

Gracious Lord, thank you for your grace and truth. Your grace truly is greater than all my sin. And your gracious truth speaks louder than all temptations, trials, and sufferings. Help me to see your grace and truth this Christmas—like the shepherds in Galilee, like the Magi from afar, and like the apostle John, I want to rejoice and say, "I have seen your glory!" In the name of the Word made flesh, amen.

DAY 14

Seeing Salvation

Now there was a man in Jerusalem, whose name was Simeon, and this man was righteous and devout, waiting for the consolation of Israel . . . and he came in the Spirit into the temple, and when the parents brought in the child Jesus, to do for him according to the custom of the Law, he took him up in his arms and blessed God and said, "Lord, now you are letting your servant depart in peace, according to your word; for my eyes have seen your salvation."

LUKE 2:25-30

When Simeon came into the temple, he saw there a little babe, and he recognized in that newly born child Jesus, the promised Savior. And as he took up that Savior into his arms, he said, "My eyes have seen"—seen what? "Your salvation"—God's salvation: not only the worker of the salvation but the salvation itself. Simeon did not say, *I think I see the salvation of God in Christ. I hope I do. Maybe I do.* No, no. He said,

"My eyes have seen your salvation." Oh, happy are you, my dear friends, if you can distinctly and clearly see in Christ Jesus the salvation of God!

It was not flesh and blood that revealed God's salvation to Simeon as he took that babe out of the arms of Mary and embraced him with eager joy. God's grace had taught him that this was the Savior. True, Christ was but a baby then, and Simeon could easily hold him in his arms; yet his faith could see everlasting salvation—infinite salvation within God incarnate. This was before our Lord had begun to preach or to teach, or to suffer for our sins; as a babe, he was God's salvation. The gospel loses very much of its sweetness when the person of Christ is placed in the background and treated as if it were a mere myth or as if it were quite a secondary consideration. Why, this is the choicest dainty of the feast—the most substantial food whereon the saints are nourished; his flesh is meat indeed, and his blood is drink indeed. Everything about our Lord is saving, but he himself is salvation. His teaching, his example, his love, his tenderness, his sufferings, and his glory—all help us, but it is his own glorious self which puts efficacy into them. Had he not been man, he could not have died, and had he not been God, his dying could not have availed for our redemption. It is what he is that gives virtue to what he does. We are bidden to come, not to his work but to himself: "Come to me, all who labor and are heavy laden" (Matthew 11:28). To him we do come, and our heart can say, "He alone is my rock and my salvation" (Psalm 62:2).

Others had seen the baby Christ with their natural eyes, but Simeon had seen, in the babe, Christ the salvation of God—not with his outward eyes but with the inward perceptions of his spirit. Simeon did not only see salvation represented in its essence, but his faith saw salvation guaranteed by the appearance of the wondrous child. Incarnation is the beginning of substitution, and substitution is the guarantee of the completion and the continuance of salvation. Simeon saw, in the presentation of Christ in the temple, a foreshadowing of his crucificial death. The time would come when he had to be brought to the altar, and no redemption would be offered for him, for he himself would have to be the price for his people. As he gazed upon the child, Simeon saw the agony and bloody sweat, the cross and passion, for he knew that the incarnate God would not shrink from anything which he had undertaken. Whether in Bethlehem's manger or on Calvary's cross or on yonder throne of glory from which he shall judge the living and the dead—wherever we see him, we see the salvation of God.

Simeon must not be allowed the monopoly of these words. I claim them too: "*My* eyes have seen your salvation." Brothers and sisters, many of you can, in a spiritual sense, use the same language. It is true that we cannot take up the infant Christ into our arms, but he is "Christ in you, the hope of glory" (Colossians 1:27). It is true that we cannot look upon him with these mortal eyes, but we have seen him with those immortal eyes which death cannot dim—the eyes of our own spirit, which have been opened by God's Holy Spirit. So, though you and I miss the outward sight of Christ, we need not regret it; it is but secondary as a privilege. If, with the inner sight, we have seen the incarnate God and accepted him as our salvation, we are blessed along with holy Simeon. We have looked unto Jesus, and we are lightened. We have beheld the Lamb of God, who takes away the sins of the world.

When Simeon took Christ up in his arms, somebody might have said, *Old man, what are you doing with the newborn King? You dare hold the incarnate God, whose name is Wonderful, Counselor, the Mighty God, the Everlasting Father, the Prince of Peace?* Yes, he dares! He takes him up in his arms; he clasps him to his heart; he rejoices over him! You, dear saints of God, who have done this long ago, do it over again! Take Christ right up into your arms, as though he were still a babe. Take him still to your heart and say, "He is everything to me—my love, my hope, my brother, this blessed incarnate God, who loved me and gave himself for me."

REFLECT

What does it mean to truly see Christ with spiritual eyes? Take a few moments to answer, "What does Christ mean to me?"

PRAY

Holy Father, the eyes of my heart see Jesus in Bethlehem, atop Golgotha, in the garden tomb, and now on heaven's throne, and I can say like Simeon, "I have seen the Lord's salvation!" King Jesus, you are the gift of grace that keeps on giving. Holy Spirit, keep my eyes ever on the Son of God: my salvation, my life, my all. Amen.

DAY 15

He Came to Save Sinners

The saying is trustworthy and deserving of full acceptance, that Christ Jesus came into the world to save sinners, of whom I am the foremost.

1 TIMOTHY 1:15

Now, this text contains the gospel in brief, and yet I may say that it contains the gospel in full. It is one of the "little Bibles," as Luther used to call them. Christ Jesus could not save men had he stayed in heaven, but he *came into the world* to save sinners. The Fall was so grievous that he had to come right down into the place of our ruin; he had to come to the dunghill that he might lift us out of it. God sat in heaven and said, "Let there be light" (Genesis 1:3), and the darkness fled before him, but he could not sit in heaven and save sinners. He comes into the world to do so; down into this polluted creation, the eternal Creator must himself descend.

Lo, there in Bethlehem's manger he sleeps, and onto a woman's breast he latches! Think how dreadful the ruin must be of us sinners when we see that Christ cannot return saying, "It is finished," until first of all he dies. That sacred head must be crowned with thorns, those eyes must be closed in the darkness of the tomb, and that body must be pierced even to its heart and then must lie a chill, cold corpse in the grave before anyone can be redeemed. Now, one of the most important questions that can be asked by anyone is this: for whom is salvation meant? The answer we have is given by the Holy Spirit in the inspired word of God: "sinners."

Christ's salvation is meant for sinners and none else. Somebody says, "But isn't that a plain matter of fact?" It is, but it is a fact scarcely ever realized. Indeed, its real meaning is not known until God the Holy Spirit reveals it. A great many persons have a notion that Christ Jesus came into the world to save respectable people who, if they have done any wrong, have repented of it and have made things square. He came, according to them, to save persons who do their very best by attendance at worship and taking the sacrament and giving to the poor and paying their way and saying their prayers. I lay down this straight line—Christ did not come into the world to save anybody but sinners. And he viewed those sinners as sinners and nothing more. He did not view them as repenting sinners nor as believing sinners nor as humble sinners nor as sanctified sinners nor as anything else but sinners, and under that character he contemplated their salvation. The text says nothing more and nothing less than that—there is not a qualifying word. It is clear that sinners only are the objects of salvation, for none but sinners need saving. And if there had been no sinners, there would certainly have been no saving and no Savior. Who wants saving but a lost man? Who wants a Savior but a man who through his sin has ruined himself? The very term "Savior" and the very name "Jesus" imply that salvation work is for sinners.

He has come, therefore, to be the anointed Savior. He was commissioned to be a Savior. And if he is not a Savior (I say it with all reverence), he is nothing. He came into the world to save, and if he does not save, he has missed his mark. He laid his heavenly glories down to take this still higher glory: that he might be the Savior of sinners. The angel of the Lord said to Joseph, "You shall call his name Jesus, for he will save his people from their sins" (Matthew 1:21). Beloved, do notice this: the Savior of sinners is not the virgin Mary. Saints are not saviors, but Christ Jesus came into the world to save sinners—the Creator of all things, sustaining all things by the word of his power. He came into the world, to Bethlehem's manger and afterwards to Calvary's cross, with this as his one business: that he might save sinners. Is he not just the Savior that we need? God and yet man in one person—he is able to sympathize because he is man, and he is able to save because he is God! Blessed God-man, Jesus Christ, you are able to save me!

Christ did not come into the world to help us save ourselves. He came to save us, not to set us on our legs and say, *Now you do so much, and I will do the rest.* No, he came to save us. From top to bottom, salvation is all grace and all the gift of God by Jesus Christ. He did not come to save us in part but in full—to have our old thoughts made into new ones; to have our old habits broken off and to have new habits given; to have our old sins pardoned and to have righteousness imputed; to have peace in the conscience, peace to man, and peace with God; to have the spotless robe of imputed righteousness cast around us and ourselves healed and cleansed. To be saved is to be rescued from the gulf of perdition; to be raised to the throne of heaven; to be delivered from the wrath and the curse and the thunders of an angry God, and brought to feel and taste the love, the approval, and the applause of Jehovah, our Father and our Friend. And all this Christ gives to sinners.

REFLECT

What edits are you prone to make to the clear and simple definition of those whom Jesus came to save? From the final paragraph, what examples of Christ's saving power help you to trust him more and more?

PRAY

My precious Savior, my heart rejoices in the reality that you came to save sinners—because that's who I am. But because of you, that's not all I am. You made me a *saved* sinner, a *forgiven* sinner, a new creation. Thank you, Lord, for coming to the fallen human race to raise us up with you. I praise your name! Amen.

DAY 16

Mary's Song

And Mary said,
"My soul magnifies the Lord,
and my spirit rejoices in God my Savior,
for he has looked on the humble
estate of his servant."

LUKE 1:46-48

This is a season when we are expected to be joyous. We greet one another with a "Merry Christmas." This is the season when we are expected to be happy, and my heart's desire is that, in the highest and best sense, you who are believers may be "merry." Observe the sacred joy of Mary that you may imitate it.

Mary's heart was merry within her, but here was the mark of her joy: it was all holy merriment. It was—every drop of it—sacred mirth. It was not such merriment as unbelievers will revel in but such merriment as the angels have around the throne, where they sing, "Glory to God in the highest," while we sing, "On earth peace among those with whom he is pleased" (Luke 2:14). Such merry hearts have a continual feast. I want you to possess today and all your days the high and consecrated bliss of Mary, that you may not only read her words but use them for yourselves, ever experiencing their meaning: "My soul magnifies the Lord, and my spirit rejoices in God my Savior."

Mary praised God with *personal devotion*. Notice how intensely personal her song is. Elizabeth is there, yet Mary sings as though she were all alone: "*My* soul magnifies the Lord, and *my* spirit rejoices in God *my* Savior." While we should join with our fellow Christians in songs of praise, we must always mind that our personal note is not omitted. "My soul"—for I have a personal indebtedness to you, my God, and there is a personal union between you and me. I love you, and you love me, and, therefore, even if all other souls are mute, "my soul magnifies the Lord." Oh, you can never know the joy of Mary unless Christ becomes truly and really yours. But oh, when he is yours—yours within—reigning in your heart, controlling all your passions, changing your nature, subduing your corruptions, inspiring you with holy emotions—a joy unspeakable and full of glory—oh then you can sing; you must sing. Who can restrain your tongue? If all the scoffers and mockers upon earth should bid you hold your peace, you must sing, for your spirit must rejoice in God your Savior.

In Mary's song we see great *spirituality*. You see how she puts this matter twice over: "My *soul* magnifies the Lord, and my *spirit* rejoices in God my Savior." She is far from being content with mere lip service. I have no doubt that her voice was exceedingly sweet, but she does not say anything about that—she speaks of "my soul" and "my spirit." O dear friends, let us never be satisfied with any kind of worship which does not take up the whole of our inner and higher nature. Who you are within is who you really are before the living God, and it is quite a secondary matter how loud the song may be or how sweet the tune of your hymn or how delightfully you join in it, unless your spirit—your soul—truly praises the Lord.

Let us bless God that our religion is not one of gloom. I do not know of a command anywhere in Scripture, *Groan in the Lord always; again I will say, groan.* From the conduct of some people, we might almost imagine that they must have altered their New Testament in that particular passage and thus woefully changed the glory of the original verse: "Rejoice in the Lord always; again I will say, rejoice" (Philippians 4:4).

If the joy of the Lord be your strength, why not express it in holy song? Why should your joys not have a tongue as well as the joys of the ungodly? When warriors win victories, they shout—have we won no victories through Jesus Christ our Lord? When people celebrate their festivals, they sing—are there any festivals equal to ours: our paschal supper, our passage of the Red Sea, our jubilee, our expectation of the coronation of our King, our hymn of victory over all the hosts of hell? Oh, surely, if the children of earth sing, the children of heaven ought to sing far more often, far more loudly, far more harmoniously than they do. Come, then, let us sing because we are glad in the Lord.

REFLECT

Lift up your voice and soul to your Lord and Savior. Find time to sing along with your favorite Christmas hymn or sing it with your family before bed.

PRAY

May my soul magnify you, my Lord! In all of the buzz, shopping, and traveling, may you be first in my heart. Satisfy my soul more than the perfect family gathering. Ignite my praise over the miraculous and merry truth that you are my God and Savior. Lord, I want you to be big, magnified, in my life. Like Mary, make me glad in you during this Christmas season—and for eternity. In Christ's name, amen.

DAY 17

Christ's Humility

Have this mind among yourselves, which is yours in Christ Jesus, who, though he was in the form of God, did not count equality with God a thing to be grasped, but emptied himself, by taking the form of a servant, being born in the likeness of men. And being found in human form, he humbled himself by becoming obedient to the point of death, even death on a cross.

PHILIPPIANS 2:5-8

You and I can have no idea of how high an honor it is to be equal with God. How can we, therefore, measure the descent of Christ when our highest thoughts cannot comprehend the height from which he came? The depth to which he descended is immeasurably below any point we have ever reached, and the height from which he came is inconceivably above our loftiest thought. Do not, however, forget the glory that Jesus laid aside for a while. The incarnation is a great marvel—that the eternal God should take into union with himself our human nature and should be born at Bethlehem and live at Nazareth and die at Calvary on our behalf.

He was the Creator, and we see him here on earth as a creature. The Creator, who made heaven and earth, without whom nothing was made, lay in the virgin's womb. He is born, and he is cradled where the oxen feed. The Creator is now a creature; the Son of God is the Son of Man—a strange combination! Could condescension go further than for the Omnipotent to join the feebleness of a newborn babe? If it had pleased him, he might have been born a man and not have been a child; he might have leaped over the period of gradual development from childhood to youth and from youth to manhood—but he did not do so. When you see him at home at Nazareth, obedient to his parents, doing the little errands of the house like any other child, you say, as our text says, "He humbled himself." There he dwelt in poverty with his parents and, I suppose, ran out to play with youthful companions. All this is very wonderful. He veiled his Godhead behind his childhood. When he went up to Jerusalem and listened to the doctors of the law, though he astonished them by his questions and answers, yet he went home with his parents and was subject to them, for "he humbled himself."

Now, let us look, with awe and reverence, at the abyss into which he descended in humility. What was the bottom of the abyss? It was death: "He humbled himself by becoming obedient to the point of death." But, as if death were not sufficiently humbling, the apostle adds, "... even death on a cross." What will Christ not do for us who have been given to him by his Father? There is no measure to his love; you cannot comprehend his grace. Oh, how we ought to love him and serve him! The lower he stoops to save us, the higher we ought to lift him in our adoring reverence. Blessed be his name; he stoops and stoops and stoops and, when he reaches our level and becomes man, he still stoops and stoops and stoops lower and deeper yet to "death on a cross."

The cross was the worst kind of death. It was a *violent death*. Jesus did not fall asleep gently, as good men often do whose end is peace. No, he died by cruel, murderous hands that took him and crucified and slew him. It was an *extremely painful death* of lingering agony. Those parts of the body in which the nerves are most numerous were pierced with rough iron nails. The weight of the body was made to hang upon the tenderest part of the frame. No doubt the nails tore their cruel way through his flesh while he was hanging on the tree. It was also a most *shameful death*. Thieves were crucified with him; his adversaries stood and mocked him. The death of the cross was reserved for slaves and the worst criminals. No Roman citizen could be put to death in such a way as that: hung up between earth and heaven as if neither would have him, rejected of men and despised of God. It was also a *penal death*. He died not like a hero in battle nor as one who perishes while rescuing someone from fire or flood—he died as a criminal. Upon the cross of Calvary, he was hung up. It was an *accursed death* too. God himself had called it so: "Cursed is everyone who is hanged on a tree" (Galatians 3:13). He was made a curse for us. His death was penal in the highest sense. He "bore our sins in his body on the tree" (1 Peter 2:24).

What I would have you learn from Christ's humiliation is this: cultivate a great hatred of sin. Sin killed Christ; let Christ kill sin. Christ was crucified; let your lusts be crucified, and let every wrong desire be nailed up with Christ upon the felon's tree. If, with Paul, you can say, "But far be it from me to boast except in the cross of our Lord Jesus Christ, by which the world has been crucified to me, and I to the world" (Galatians 6:14), with him you will also be able to exclaim, "From now on let no one cause me trouble, for I bear on my body the marks of Jesus" (Galatians 6:17).

O beloved, when we have meditated on this story of Christ's humbling himself, we ought to feel our love to our Lord growing very passionate! We do not half love him as we ought. Come, seek his wounds, and let your hearts be wounded. Come, look to his heart, which poured out blood and water, and give your heart up to him. Put your whole being now among the sweet spices of his all-sufficient merit, set all on fire with burning affection, and let the fragrance of it go up like incense before the Lord.

REFLECT

What arises in your heart as you meditate on the humility of Christ? What sins do you need to believe have been crucified with Christ?

PRAY

Lord Jesus, I cannot fully comprehend how the eternal Son of God became a human—but I thank you. And yet, you humbled yourself even more by dying on the cross for my wickedness. This is why Christmas is merry! Mercy of mercies, you came to redeem me. May your cross-shaped humility capture and form my heart and mind in this busy season. Thank you, Jesus. Amen.

DAY 18

In a Manger

And she gave birth to her firstborn son and wrapped him in swaddling cloths and laid him in a manger, because there was no place for them in the inn.

LUKE 2:7

Let me lead your meditations to the stable at Bethlehem that you may see this great sight—the Savior in the manger—and think over the reason for this lowly crib: "because there was no place for them in the inn."

When his mother swaddled him, she laid him in the manger. He was not like those who are born in marble halls and are wrapped in scarlet, but he was a poor commoner, and he took a lowly place even in his birth. He came, according to prophecy, to be "despised and rejected by men, a man of sorrows and acquainted with grief" (Isaiah 53:3); and he was to have "no form or majesty"—"a root out of a dry ground" (v 2). Would it have been fitting for the man who was to die naked on the cross to be robed in purple at his birth? Would it not have been inappropriate that the Redeemer who was to be buried in a borrowed tomb should be born anywhere but in the humblest shed, and housed anywhere but in the most ignoble manner? The manger and the cross standing at the two extremes of the Savior's earthly life seem most fit and congruous to each other. He stooped to lift us up. He made the heavens, and yet he lay in Bethlehem's manger. He hung the stars in their places and laid the beams of the universe, and yet he became a carpenter's son, giving up all his rank and dignity for love's dear sake. Love fetched him from his throne in heaven; love disrobed him of his glories; love laid him in Bethlehem's manger; love led him through this weary world for 33 years; love took him to Gethsemane; love oppressed him till he sweat great drops of blood; love made him bow his head and give up the ghost that he might redeem his people from their sins.

In being laid in a manger, he did, as it were, give an invitation to the most lowly and sinful to come to him. We might tremble to approach a throne, but we cannot fear to approach a manger. Even as an infant, by being laid in a manger, he was set forth as the sinner's friend. Come to him, you who are weary and heavy laden! Come to him, you that are broken in spirit, who are bowed down in soul! Come to him, you that despise yourselves and are despised by others! Come to him, you cheats and immoral ones! Come to him, crooks and drunks! In the manger, there he lies, unguarded from your touch and unshielded from your gaze. Bow the knee and kiss the Son of God. Accept him as your Savior, for he puts himself into that manger that you may approach him. The throne of Solomon might awe you, but the manger of the Son of David must invite you.

This brings me to the most necessary application to dwell upon for a moment. Do you have room for Christ? Have you a place for him in your heart? You may say, "Oh, but I feel it is a place not at all fit for Christ!" Nor was the manger a place fit for him, and yet there was he laid. "Oh, but I have been such a sinner. I feel as if my heart had been a den of beasts and devils!" Well, the manger had been a place where beasts had fed. Have you room for him? Never mind what the past has been—he can forget and forgive. Oh, it shall be a happy day for you if you shall be enabled to take him in your arms and receive him as the consolation of Israel!

My Master wants room! I, his herald, cry aloud: "Room for the Savior! Here is my royal Master—have you a place for him? Here is the Son of God made flesh—have you room for him? Here is he who can forgive all sin—have you room for him? Here is he who can take you up out of the horrible pit and out of the miry clay—have you room for him? Here is he who will abide with you forever to make your heart a heaven of joy and bliss—have you room for him? It's all I ask. Your emptiness, your nothingness, your lack of feeling, your lack of goodness, your need of grace—all these will be but room for him. Have you room for him?" O Spirit of God, lead many readers to say, "Yes, my heart is ready." Ah, then he will come and dwell with you.

REFLECT

What are the areas of your life where you think there's no place for Christ? Where do you need to invite his gracious redeeming presence and power?

PRAY

Lord Jesus, you went from angels arrayed around you in praise to cattle around you as you lay where they graze. Your humble birth showed how you treat us sinners—you draw near, you are kind, you came to save. Lord, help me to get low enough to see your great grace and respond in lifelong praise. In your name, Jesus, amen.

DAY 19

Great Joy

And in the same region there were shepherds out in the field, keeping watch over their flock by night. And an angel of the Lord appeared to them, and the glory of the Lord shone around them, and they were filled with great fear. And the angel said to them, "Fear not, for behold, I bring you good news of great joy that will be for all the people. For unto you is born this day in the city of David a Savior, who is Christ the Lord."

LUKE 2:8-11

The birth of Christ should be the subject of supreme joy. We have the angelic reason for rejoicing because Christ is born. It is a truth so full of joy that it caused the angel who came to announce it to be filled with gladness. The joy which this first gospel preacher spoke of was no small joy, for he said, "I bring you good news of great joy." Every word is emphatic, as if to show that the gospel is above all things intended to promote—and most abundantly create—the greatest possible joy in the human heart wherever it is received.

So glad were the angels at this gospel that after one angel evangelized and gave out the gospel, suddenly a band of them appeared and sang an anthem loud and sweet that there might be a full service at the first propounding of the glad tidings of great joy. A multitude of the heavenly host had heard that a chosen messenger had been sent to proclaim the newborn King and, filled with holy joy and adoration, they gathered up their strength to pursue him, for they could not let him go to earth alone on such an errand. They overtook him just as he had reached the last word of his announcement, and then they broke forth in that famous chorale: the only one sung by angels that was ever heard by human ears here below. It was so glad a message that they could not let it be simply spoken by even an angel's solitary voice, but they must pour forth a glad chorus of praise, singing unto the Lord a new song:

> *"Glory to God in the highest, and on earth peace, among those with whom he is pleased!" (Luke 2:14)*

Brothers and sisters, if the birth of Jesus was so gladsome to our cousins the angels, what should it be to us? If it made the angels sing, who had comparatively so small a share in it, how should it make us leap for joy? Oh, if it brought heaven down to earth, should not our songs go up to heaven? If heaven's gate of pearl was set open at its widest, and a stream of shining ones came running downward to the lower skies, to anticipate the time when they shall all descend in solemn pomp at the glorious advent of the great King… if it emptied heaven for a while to make earth so glad, ought not our thoughts and praises and all our loves to go pouring up to the eternal gate, leaving earth a while that we may crowd heaven with the songs of mortal men? Yes, truly, so let it be.

"Glory to the newborn King!"
Let us all the anthem sing,
"Peace on earth, and mercy mild;
God and sinners reconciled."[5]

What joy there is in this! Oh, that our hearts were but half alive to the incarnation! Oh, that we did but know a thousandth of the unutterable delight which is hidden in this thought: that the Son of God was born a man at Bethlehem! Thus you see that there is overflowing cause for joy in the birth of Christ because it was the incarnation of the Deity.

The angel explained our cause for joy by saying that he who was born unto us was a Savior. Brothers and sisters, I know who will be gladdest today to think that Christ was born a Savior—it will be those who are most conscious of their sinnership. If you know you are lost by nature and lost by practice, if you feel sin like a plague in your heart, if evil wearies and worries you, if you have known of iniquity the burden and the shame, then will it be bliss to you even to hear of that Savior whom the Lord has provided. Even as a baby, Jesus the Savior will be precious to you, but most of all because he has now finished all the work of your salvation. He is a Savior by birth—for this purpose is he born. To save sinners is his birthright and office.

Is there not joy in this? Where else is there joy if not here? You cannot see with the physical eye, but you must meditate and so see with the mental eye this great and grand and glorious truth: that the Word was made flesh and dwelt among us. This is the way to have joy today—joy as it fitly descends from heaven with the descent of heaven's King. Believe, draw near, and then fixedly gaze upon him and so be blessed. Express your joy, as the angels did. Sing then your anthems, and praise God with all your hearts, and lift up your joyful hymns unto the newborn King. Come and worship God manifest in the flesh and be filled with his light and sweetness by the power of the Holy Spirit.

REFLECT

What would it look like for you to express "great joy" over Jesus today? Ask the Spirit to reveal and remove anything that is clogging or clouding your joy in your Savior.

PRAY

Offer up a prayer of praise and joy. Say as many things that come to mind in this format: "Lord, your incarnation gives me great joy because..."

DAY 20

He Became Poor

For you know the grace of our Lord Jesus Christ, that though he was rich, yet for your sake he became poor, so that you by his poverty might become rich.

2 CORINTHIANS 8:9

Christ's coming from heaven to earth to suffer for us is here called "grace." The kindness, the bounty, the benevolence, the generosity, the compassion, the condescension, the tenderness, "the *grace* of our Lord Jesus Christ." It was an act of grace on his part—an act purely gratuitous. He was not bound to have done it. We did not deserve it at his hands. It was no merit of ours foreseen, or of any other kind, to draw him from the skies and drag him to the manger and the tomb. But he came as an act of free mercy to undeserving sinners. Grace was the source and fountain of his coming. That eternal love of God, by which we were first chosen, was the same love that sent the Savior to redeem the chosen. It was that grace from which all covenant mercies spring—the ancient wellhead of distinguishing grace—which brought the Savior here.

The apostle Paul follows it up by mentioning the heights from which the Savior descended: "though he was rich." This little clause is clear proof that our Savior existed before he was born into this world—that, in fact, he was divine. Do not think that our Savior began to live when he was born of the virgin Mary; don't imagine that he dates his existence from the manger at Bethlehem. Remember, he is the eternal, he is before all things, and by him all things consist. There was never a time when he was not God. He is self-existent, with no beginning of days or end of years; he is the immortal, invisible, only wise God, our Savior.

Oh, how surprised the angels were when they were first informed that Jesus Christ, the Prince of light and majesty, intended to shroud himself in clay and become a babe, and live and die! We know not how it was first mentioned to the angels, but when the rumor first began to get afloat among the sacred hosts, you may imagine the strange wonderment. "Is it true that he whose crown is all adorned with stars would lay that crown aside? What! Could it be true that he who is everlasting and immortal would one day be nailed to a cross?" Oh, how their wonderment increased! And when the Son of God descended from on high, they followed him, for Jesus was "seen by angels" (1 Timothy 3:16), and seen in a special sense—they looked upon him in rapturous amazement, wondering what it all could mean.

Oh, can you conceive the yet increasing wonder of the heavenly hosts when the deed was actually done, when they saw the crown taken off? Can you conceive it, when he said to them, *I do not disdain the womb of the virgin; I am going down to earth to become a man*? Can you picture the angels as they declared they would follow him? Yes, they followed him as near as he would permit them. And when they came to earth, they began to sing, "Glory to God in the highest" (Luke 2:14). Nor would the angels go away till they had made the shepherds wonder and till heaven had hung out new stars in honor of the newborn King. And now, wonder how he upon whose shoulders the universe hangs, who created all things, has now become so weak that a woman must carry him! Oh, for words to picture the humility and poverty of Christ!

Why did the Savior become poor? The Scripture says, "For your sake." I want you, if it is true, to say, "For my sake, out of love to me, Jesus Christ left his throne in heaven to die on the cross of Calvary." Take this truth to yourself: Jesus Christ loved you and gave himself for you, as much as if nobody else had ever lived. You have been lifted so high because he was dragged down so low; you have been filled because he was emptied; you live because he died. As you think of your innumerable mercies, remember that every one has his blood upon it. For if Jesus Christ died for you, you are rich through that which is imputed to you—for all that Jesus had and did is yours. His matchless righteousness is yours; you have it on already if you are a believer, and so you are arrayed in fair white linen. His atonement is yours; his precious blood has washed all your guilt away; you are without spot even before the eye of the all-seeing one. The great economy of grace with all its fullness is yours. Remember that adoption, justification, and sanctification are all yours. You have everything the heart can want in spiritual things. You are rich with true riches and not with the riches of a dream, but yours are everlasting treasures; yours are solid riches. Does not your very heart sing as you try to realize how rich you are and how rich you shall be forever? Christ in his poverty should be a most common object of our contemplation, for it is through that poverty that we have been made rich.

REFLECT

How has Christ's becoming poor made you rich? What spiritual riches from Christ are you most enjoying?

PRAY

Holy Spirit, help me to know the grace of the Lord Jesus more fully this Advent season. Jesus, you exchanged a throne for a manger, heaven's crown for a cross, the attention of the angels for the scorn of the world, honor for shame, and glory for my sin—and you did this for my sake. Oh, come, let us adore him, Christ the Lord!

DAY 21

Grace Appeared

For the grace of God has appeared, bringing salvation for all people, training us to renounce ungodliness and worldly passions, and to live self-controlled, upright, and godly lives in the present age, waiting for our blessed hope, the appearing of the glory of our great God and Savior Jesus Christ, who gave himself for us to redeem us from all lawlessness and to purify for himself a people for his own possession who are zealous for good works.

TITUS 2:11-14

When the Lord Jesus Christ came to Bethlehem and when he closed a perfect life by death upon Calvary, he manifested the grace of God more gloriously than has been done by creation or providence. This is the clearest revelation of the everlasting mercy of the living God.

We live in an age that is an interval between two appearances of the Lord from heaven. Believers in Jesus are shut off from the old economy by the first coming of our Lord. We are divided from the past by a wall of light upon whose forefront we read the words: Bethlehem, Gethsemane, Calvary. We date our years from the birth of the virgin's son, so we begin with AD, *Anno Domini,* which means, "In the year of our Lord". Bethlehem's manger is our beginning. To us, the chief landmark in all time is the wondrous life of him who is the light of the world. We look to the appearing of the grace of God in the form of the lowly one of Nazareth, for our trust is there. We confide in him who was made flesh and dwelt among us and whose first disciples beheld his glory, the glory as of the only begotten of the Father, full of grace and truth. The dense darkness of the pagan ages begins to be broken when we reach the first appearing, and the dawn of a glorious day begins.

Brothers and sisters, we also look forward to a second appearing. We believe that our Lord, in the fullness of time, will descend from heaven with a shout, with the trump of the archangel and the voice of God. This is the terminus of the present age. We look from *Anno Domini,* in which he came the first time, to that greater *Anno Domini,* or year of our Lord, in which he shall come a second time, in all the splendor of his power, to reign in righteousness and break the evil powers as with a rod of iron.

See, then, where we are: we are compassed about, behind, and before with the appearings of our Lord. Behind us is our trust; before us is our hope. Behind us is the Son of God in humiliation; before us is the great God our Savior in his glory. To use an ecclesiastical term, we stand between two epiphanies. The first is the manifestation of the Son of God in human flesh in dishonor and weakness. The second is the manifestation of the same Son of God in all his power and glory. In what a position, then, do the saints stand! They have an era all to themselves which begins and ends with the Lord's appearing.

Then come the tender thoughts—the memories of what the Lord has done for us to make us holy: redemption with a wondrous price. Behold how the Lord Jesus loved us and gave himself for us. O readers, if nothing else can touch our hearts, this must: "You are not your own, for you were bought with a price" (1 Corinthians 6:19-20).

And he gave himself for us with these two objects: first, *redemption*, that he might redeem us from all iniquity—that he might break the bonds of sin asunder and cast the cords of depravity far from us. He died—never forget it!—that your sins might die. He died that every lust might be dragged into captivity at his chariot wheels. Next, he died that he may *purify* us unto himself—as the Hebrew would put it—to be his *segullah*: his "treasured possession" (Exodus 19:5). Believers are Christ's own people—his choice and select portion. Saints are Christ's crown jewels; his box of diamonds; his very, very, very own. He carries his people as lambs close to his chest; he engraves their names on his heart. They are the inheritance to which he is the heir, and he values them more than all the universe besides. He would lose everything else sooner than lose one of them. He desires that you who are being trained by his grace should know that you are altogether his. You are Christ's. You are, each one, to feel, "I do not belong to the world; I do not belong to myself; I belong only to Christ. I am set aside by him for himself only, and his I will be." The silver and the gold are his, and the cattle upon a thousand hills are his; but he makes small account of them—"The LORD's portion is his people" (Deuteronomy 32:9).

REFLECT

How is the return of Christ, his second advent, shaping your life today? How does Christ's first appearing, in order to make you his treasure, expand the way you view Christmas?

PRAY

Lord Jesus, as this season is meant to remind me of your first appearing, help me not to forget that you will appear again. You are surely returning soon! Fine-tune my heart to respond in joy to the double gift—your incarnation and your return! May your second advent also cause me to long for Immanuel, God with us, and to sing, "Let earth receive her King!"[6] Come quickly, Lord Jesus. Amen.

DAY 22

Responding to the Redeemer

When the angels went away from them into heaven, the shepherds said to one another, "Let us go over to Bethlehem and see this thing that has happened, which the Lord has made known to us." And they went with haste and found Mary and Joseph, and the baby lying in a manger. And when they saw it, they made known the saying that had been told them concerning this child. And all who heard it wondered at what the shepherds told them. But Mary treasured up all these things, pondering them in her heart. And the shepherds returned, glorifying and praising God for all they had heard and seen, as it had been told them.

LUKE 2:15-20

Every season has its own proper fruit—apples for autumn, holly berries for Christmas. And, at this season, when the world is engaged in congratulating itself and in expressing its complimentary wishes for the good of its citizens, let me suggest a more solid work for Christians. As we think today of the birth of the Savior, let us aspire to a fresh birth of the Savior in our hearts, that we may go again to the Bethlehem of our spiritual nativity and do our first works, enjoy our first loves, and feast with Jesus as we did in those first holy, happy, heavenly days of our conversion.

First, let us celebrate Christmas with holy wonder, admiration, and adoration. "And all who heard it wondered at what the shepherds told them." Let me suggest to you that holy wonder at what God has done should be very natural to you. That God should consider his fallen creature, and, instead of sweeping it away in destruction, God should devise a wonderful redemption, and that he should himself undertake to be our Redeemer and to pay the ransom price—this is, indeed, marvelous! It is most marvelous to you in its relation to yourself: that *you* should be redeemed by blood—that God should forsake the thrones and royalties above to suffer shame below for *you*. Let your soul lose itself in wonder, for wonder, dear friends, is in this way a very practical emotion.

Holy wonder will lead you to grateful worship; being astonished at what God has done, you will pour out your soul with astonishment at the foot of the golden throne with the song, "To him who sits on the throne and to the Lamb be blessing and honor and glory and might forever and ever!" (Revelation 5:13). Who can be astonished at anything more when you have been astonished at the manger and the cross? What is there wonderful left after one has seen the Savior? There is more of God to be seen in the manger and the cross than in the sparkling stars above, the rolling deep below, the towering mountains, the teeming valleys, the abodes of life, or the abyss of death. Let us then spend some choice hours of this festive season in holy wonder that will produce gratitude, worship, love, and confidence.

A second manner of holy work is found in Mary's sacred heart, pondering and preserving. "Mary treasured up all these things, pondering them in her heart." Observe the exercise of this blessed woman in the three great parts of her being. Her memory—she treasured all these things; her affections—she kept them in her heart; her intellect—she pondered them, considered them, weighed them, and turned them over; so that memory, affection, and understanding were all exercised in regard to these things. Beloved, remember what you have heard of Christ and what he has done for you. Make your heart the golden cup to hold the rich recollections of his past loving-kindness; make it a pot of manna to preserve the heavenly bread whereon saints have fed in days gone by. Let your memory treasure up everything about Christ which you have either heard or felt or known, and then let your fond affections hold him fast evermore. Love him! Pour out that alabaster box of your heart and let all the precious ointment of your affection come streaming on his feet. Love the blessed Son of God, your ever-tender friend. Let your intellect be exercised concerning the Lord Jesus. Turn over and over in meditation what you read.

O beloved, here is a blessed Christmas work for you if, like Mary, you lay up all these things in your heart and ponder upon them.

"The shepherds returned," we read in the 20th verse, "glorifying and praising God for all they had heard and seen, as it had been told them." The way these shepherds honored God is worth noting. They did it by praising him. Let us think more of sacred song than we sometimes do. Sing then, my brothers and sisters! Sing not only when you are together but sing alone. Praise God that you hear there is a Savior! Praise God that you hear that the plan of salvation is very simple! Praise God that you have a Savior for your own soul! Praise God that you are pardoned—that you are saved! Praise him for what you have heard, but observe how the shepherds also praised God for what they had seen. Look at the 20th verse: "heard and seen." There is the sweetest music—what we have experienced, what we have felt within, what we have made our own. Mere hearing may make some music, but the soul of song must come from seeing with the eye of faith.

Observe the last clause: "as it had been told them." Have you not found the gospel to be in yourselves just what the Bible said it would be? Jesus said he would give you grace—have you not had it? He promised you rest—have you not received it? He said that you should have joy and comfort and life through believing in him—have you not had all these? Are not his ways ways of pleasantness and his paths paths of peace? I have found Christ sweeter than his servants could set him forth as being. May you keep and celebrate this season in holy contemplation and in blessed service of that gracious God whose unspeakable gift to us is the newborn King.

REFLECT

Spend a few moments in silent meditation on the wonderful and marvelous gift of Christ to you this Christmas.

PRAY

Lord Jesus, you are the reason why this season is so lovely, so wonderful, so marvelous. May the gospel truth of Christmas recalibrate the remainder of the season. Refresh my soul with the smell of grace. Revive my heart with the wonder of your incarnation. Retune my singing to you because you are worthy to be praised. Make me happy in you, Lord, for I have heard and seen your goodness! In your name, King Jesus, amen.

DAY 23

The Wise Men

Now after Jesus was born in Bethlehem of Judea in the days of Herod the king, behold, wise men from the east came to Jerusalem, saying, "Where is he who has been born king of the Jews? For we saw his star when it rose and have come to worship him."… When they saw the star, they rejoiced exceedingly with great joy. And going into the house, they saw the child with Mary his mother, and they fell down and worshiped him. Then, opening their treasures, they offered him gifts, gold and frankincense and myrrh.

MATTHEW 2:1–2, 10–11

A stir begins as soon as Christ is born. He has not spoken a word, he has not wrought a miracle, he has not proclaimed a single doctrine; but "Jesus was born." And though you hear nothing but infant cries and see nothing but infant weakness, still his influence upon the world is manifest. There is infinite power even in an infant Savior. Jesus of Nazareth is so potent a factor in the world that no sooner is he there in his utmost weakness, a newborn King, than he begins to reign.

The incarnation of the Son of God was one of the greatest events in the history of the universe. Its actual occurrence was not, however, known to all mankind but was specially revealed to the shepherds of Bethlehem and to certain wise men—Magi, students of the stars and of old prophetic books from the far-off east. We will now endeavor to learn a practical lesson from the story of the wise men who came from the east to worship Christ. If God the Holy Spirit shall teach us, we may gather such instruction that may lead us also to become worshipers of the Savior and joyful believers in him.

These wise men came to Jesus, and in so doing, they did three things: they saw, they worshiped, and they gave. Those are three things which every believer may do and which every seeker should do for the first time. First, they saw the young child. I do not think they merely said, *There he is,* and so ended the matter, but they stood still and looked. Perhaps for some minutes they did not speak. They gazed with all their eyes. They looked and looked and looked again. They glanced at his mother, but they fixed their eyes on him. "They saw the child." So, too, today, let us think of Jesus with fixed and continuous thought. He is God; he is man; he is the substitute for sinners. He is willing to receive all who trust him. He will save, and save this day, every one of us who will rely upon him.

Bring him before your mind's eye; consider and admire him. Is it not a wonder that God should enter into union with man and come to this world as an infant? For our redemption, the Word was made flesh. This truth will breed the brightest hope within your soul. Though it is many a year since I first looked to him, I desire to look to Jesus again. The incarnate God! My eyes swim with tears to think that he who might have crushed me into hell forever becomes a young child for my sake.

What did the wise men do next? They worshiped him. Beloved readers, if wise men of old came to Jesus and worshiped, should we not also? My intense desire is that we all may pay homage to him of whom we sing, "For to us a child is born, to us a son is given" (Isaiah 9:6). Let those of us who have long worshiped him worship anew with yet lowlier reverence and intenser love. These wise men came naturally, traversing the desert; let us come spiritually, leaving our sins. The sight of a star guided them; let us be guided by faith in the divine Spirit, by the teaching of his word, and by all those blessed lights which the Lord uses to conduct men and women to himself. Only let us come to Jesus. It was well to come unto the babe Jesus, led by the feeble beams of a star; you shall find it still more blessed to come to him now that he is exalted in the highest heavens and by his own light reveals his own perfect glory. Delay not, for this day he cries, "Come to me, all who labor and are heavy laden, and I will give you rest" (Matthew 11:28). When you think of Jesus Christ—whose goings forth were from everlasting, the eternally begotten Son of the Father—and then see him coming here to be a man of the substance of his mother, and know and understand why he came and what he did when he came, then you will fall down and worship him. Our faith sees him go from the manger to the cross, and from the cross right up to the throne; the very man who slept at Bethlehem in the manger—there he reigns as Lord of lords.

We should spend much time in worshiping the Christ, and he should always have the highest place in our reverence. Enter the house and worship! Jesus was born that you might be born again. He lived that you might live. He died that you might die to sin. He is risen, and today he makes intercession for transgressors that they may be reconciled to God through him. Come, then, and believe, trust, rejoice, adore! If you have neither gold, frankincense, nor myrrh, bring your faith, your love, and your repentance and, falling down before the Son of God, pay him the reverence of your hearts. Give him your voice—speak of him; give him your hands—work for him; give him your whole self. I know you will, for he loved you and gave himself for you. The Lord bless you and may this Christmas be a very memorable one.

REFLECT

How does the birth of Christ stir your heart and soul to worship God? How could you worship him today?

PRAY

Offer up a prayer of adoration, mentioning as many things that come to mind in this format: "Lord Jesus, I worship you because..."

DAY 24

He is Given

For to us a child is born, to us a son is given…

ISAIAH 9:6

A child! What can that do? A child! It totters in its walk; it trembles in its steps. And it is a child newly born. Born! An infant deriving its nourishment from a woman—this can work wonders? Yes, says the prophet: "For to us a child is born." But then it is added, "To us a son is given." The careful reader will soon discover a distinction, and it is not a distinction without difference. "For to us a child is *born*, to us a son is *given*."

As Jesus Christ was a child in his human nature, he was *born*, begotten of the Holy Ghost, born of the virgin Mary. He was as truly born, as certainly a child, as any other man that ever lived upon the face of the earth. He was thus, in his humanity, a child born. But as God's Son, he is not born but *given*; begotten of his Father from before all worlds. Begotten, not made—being of the same substance with the Father. The doctrine of the eternal generation of Christ[7] is to be received as an undoubted truth of our holy religion. As well might a gnat seek to drink in the ocean as a finite creature to comprehend the eternal God. A God whom we could understand would be no God. If we could grasp him, he could not be infinite; if we could understand him, then he would not be divine. He was not born in this world as God's Son, but he was sent, or was given, so that you clearly perceive that the distinction conveys much good truth to us.

But we do receive it as a fact, more fully established than any other fact in history, that the Son of God became man, was born at Bethlehem, wrapped in swaddling clothes, and laid in a manger. It is a fact, too, that "a son is given." About that, we have no question. The unbeliever may dispute, but we, professing to be believers in Scripture, receive it as an undeniable truth: that God has given his only begotten Son to be the Savior of men. God in our nature can mean nothing but joy for us. How favored is our human race in this respect! What other creature did the Lord become? We know that he did not take up angels, but he took up the seed of Abraham; he took upon himself human nature. He who was made a little lower than the angels for the suffering of death is this day crowned with glory and honor and made to have dominion over all the works of Jehovah's hands. This is the gospel indeed. Do not sinners begin to hope? Is there one in your nature who is "Light of lights, very God of very God,"[8] and do you not perceive that this means good to you? Does not the "Word [become] flesh" (John 1:14) dwelling among us ignite hope in your heart and lead you to believe that you may yet be saved?

But *the* matter in question is this: is this child born to *you?* Is he given to *you?* Do you have a personal interest in the child that was born at Bethlehem? Do you know that he is your Savior—that he has brought glad tidings to you? That to *us* he belongs? And that we belong to him? God gives him; we take him. He is born; we take him up in our arms and feel ready to cry, "Lord, now you are letting your servant depart in peace, according to your word; for my eyes have seen your salvation" (Luke 2:29-30). Shall we not accept this gift of gifts and love him because he has first loved us? To believe is to take freely what God gives freely. It is the simplest thing that can be. If you want Christ, you may have him. If you desire to have God with you, he waits to be gracious unto you. If you wish for Immanuel, behold him in Jesus, your Lord. *Oh, but I wish I had some sign that I might be sure!* What sign do you want beyond the gift of God, the birth of Jesus? Away with demands which are wild and ungenerous. The Word of God bids you believe and live. The moment you believe in Jesus, he is yours. Say, then, today, "For to us a child is born, to us a son is given," and say it with the fullness of delight.

Ah, Christians, ring the bells of your hearts, fire the salute of your most joyous songs, "For to us a child is born, to us a son is given." Dance, O my heart, and ring out peals of gladness! You drops of blood within my veins, dance every one of you! O all my nerves, become harp strings and let gratitude touch you with angelic fingers! And you, my tongue, shout—shout to his praise, who has said, "For to [you] a child is born, to [you] a son is given."

REFLECT

What does the distinction of a child *born* and a son *given* reveal about the Lord Jesus? Are you given to Christ? Is there anything you are holding back from him?

PRAY

Holy Father, you know the many concerns, worries, and anxieties of my life. Make the gospel truth of this Christmas child born to me—the Son of God given to me—remake my heart to resound with joy that surpasses all understanding. Strengthen my sense of forgiveness of sins, new life, and belonging to the one who was a child born and a son given. In the name of Jesus, amen.

DAY 25

Merry Christmas!

And she gave birth to her firstborn son and wrapped him in swaddling cloths and laid him in a manger.

LUKE 2:7

Oh, joy, joy, joy! There was born into this world a man who is also God. No other man ever had such a birthday as Jesus Christ. Of whom had prophets and seers ever written as they wrote of him? Whose name is graven on so many tablets as his? Who had such a scroll of prophecy, all pointing to him as Jesus Christ, the God-man? When did God ever hang a fresh lamp in the sky to announce the birth of anyone but Christ? When did angels ever stoop from heaven and sing choral symphonies on the birth of a mighty man? No, all others are passed by, but see in heaven there is a great light shining, and a song is heard: "Glory to God in the highest" (Luke 2:14).

The sure hope of sinners and the great joy of saints is the incarnate Lord, Immanuel, "God with us." May he be your joy and mine this day. Ring these words again: "God with us." Oh, it is one of the bells of heaven. Let us strike it yet again: "God with us." Oh, it is a stray note from the sonnets of paradise. Tell it, tell it, tell it—this is the name of him who "is born this day" (v 11). Yes, this is the solid truth upon which we plant our feet. Jesus of Nazareth is God; he who was conceived in the womb of the virgin and laid in Bethlehem's manger is now, and always was, God over all, blessed forever. There is no gospel if he be not God. It is no news to me that a great prophet is born. There have been great prophets before, but the world has never been redeemed from evil by mere testimony to the truth, and it never will be. Tell me that God is born—that God himself has espoused our nature and taken it into union with himself; then the bells of my heart ring merry peals, for now I may come to God since God has come to me.

How shall I speak of what God the Son has done for us? Think of the glory that he left and of the shame that he endured for our sakes. Let your eye lovingly gaze upon him in the weakness of his infancy and then in the greater weakness of his death-agony, and remember that he suffered all this for you. For you, the crown of thorns, the nails, the tomb—all for you. What wisdom is manifested in the plan of redemption, of which the incarnate God is the center! What love is revealed there! What power it is that brought the divine one down from glory to the manger; only omnipotence could have worked so great a marvel! What faithfulness to ancient promises! What truthfulness in keeping covenant! All the attributes of God were in that little child most marvelously displayed and veiled. Think of it: the heir of all things cradled in a manger! Look at him now, with the adoring eyes of your reverent contemplation, in his glorious deity and his perfect humanity. Look at him in the manger; behold him on the cross; regard his perfect life and his redeeming death; behold him in his resurrection, his triumphant ascension, and his perpetual intercession; and look forward to his promised return from heaven. Beloved believer, he is yours—all yours. The source of our present comfort and of our future perseverance is the fact that Jesus Christ is ours.

Now, a happy Christmas to you all! And it will be a happy Christmas if you have God with you. For my part, I wish there were 20 Christmas days in the year. I shall say nothing today against festivities on this great birthday of Christ. Feast, Christians, feast—you have a right to feast. Go to the house of feasting and celebrate your Savior's birth. But, in your feasting, think of the man in Bethlehem; let him have a place in your hearts. Give him the glory; think of the virgin who conceived him, but think most of all of the man born, the child given. Oh, what a happy Christmas that will make! May God give you peace; may he give you goodwill towards all your friends, your enemies, and your neighbors, and may he give you grace to give glory to God in the highest. I wish every one of you the happiest Christmas you ever had in your lives. I finish by again saying:

A HAPPY CHRISTMAS TO YOU ALL!

REFLECT

Have you been found by the Lord Jesus? Look to him and to his work for you and trust him to save you. If you have been saved by Jesus, how are you enjoying the freedom and comforts he's purchased for you?

PRAY

Jesus, my heart is full on this Christmas day. As I remember and marvel at your incarnation—why you came and what you suffered for me—my heart cries, thank you, Lord. I can't help but join the angel choir and out-sing them because you saved me from my sin: "Glory to God in the highest!" Glory to the newborn King! All hail King Jesus, born so we can be born again, died so we can live, and lives again so we can live with him. God with us! Hallelujah! In your name, Jesus, amen.

APPENDIX

If you are interested in reading the sermons I drew upon for these devotionals, this appendix will point you to the corresponding sermons from Spurgeon. While Spurgeon's sermons are widely available online, you may find the search bar at Spurgeon.org to be a simple way to look for them. "The Spurgeon Archive" at romans45.org also has Spurgeon's sermons listed in alphabetical order.

DAY 1

"Immanuel—the Light of Life"
"Christ Our Passover"
"The Birth of Christ"

DAY 2

"The Serpent's Sentence"
"Christ the Conqueror of Satan"
"Forgiveness"

DAY 3

"The Works of the Devil Destroyed"
"Resistance to Salvation"
"The Strong One Driven Out by a Stronger One"

DAY 4

"The Incarnation and Birth of Christ"

DAY 5

"The Mysteries of the Brazen Serpent"

DAY 6

"Sin Condemned and Executed by Christ Jesus"
"How God Condemned Sin"
"The Law's Failure and Fulfillment"

DAY 7

"He Shall Be Great"

DAY 8

"None but Jesus"
"Immeasurable Love"

DAY 9

"Jesus"

DAY 10

"Immanuel—the Light of Life"
"His Name—Wonderful!"
"Christ's Motive and Ours"

DAY 11

"God with Us"
"God Is with Us"

DAY 12
"A Personal Application"
"Jehovah Tsidkenu: The Lord Our Righteousness"

DAY 13
"The True Tabernacle, and Its Glory of Grace and Peace"
"Soul-Satisfying Bread"
"The Holy Child, Jesus"
"The Glory of Christ—Beheld!"

DAY 14
"Simeon's Swan Song"
"Nunc Dimittis"
"Christ Seen as God's Salvation"
"Thy Salvation"

DAY 15
"The Glorious Gospel"
"The Whole Gospel in a Single Verse"
"The Faithful Saying"

DAY 16
"The Key-Note of a Choice Sonnet"
"Mary's Magnificat"
"A Harp of Ten Strings"
"Mary's Song"

DAY 17
"Our Lord in the Valley of Humiliation"

DAY 18

"Our Lord's Voluntary Poverty"
"The Sad Plight and Sure Relief"
"No Room for Christ in the Inn"
"The Saviour Resting in His Love"

DAY 19

"The Great Birthday"
"Joy Born at Bethlehem"

DAY 20

"Knowing and Doing"
"The Condescension of Christ"
"Our Lord's Voluntary Poverty"
"Christ's Motive and Ours"

DAY 21

"The Two Appearings and the Discipline of Grace"

DAY 22

"Holy Work for Christmas"

DAY 23

"The Star and the Wise Men"
"The Far-Off, Near; The Near, Far Off"
"The Sages, the Star, and the Savior"

DAY 24

"A Christmas Question"
"Christ in You"

DAY 25

"The Birth of Christ"
"Going Home—a Christmas Sermon"
"The First Christmas Carol"
"The Great Birthday"
"Immanuel—the Light of Life"
"God Incarnate, the End of Fear"
"What We Have, and Are to Have"
"The Saints' Love to God"

THE NICENE CREED[9]

I believe in one God, the Father Almighty,
Maker of heaven and earth,
and of all things visible and invisible.

And in one Lord Jesus Christ,
the only-begotten Son of God,
begotten of the Father before all worlds;
God of God, Light of Light, very God of very God;
begotten, not made,
being of one substance with the Father,
by whom all things were made.
Who, for us men and for our salvation,
came down from heaven
and was incarnate by the Holy Spirit
of the Virgin Mary,
and was made man;
and was crucified also for us under Pontius Pilate;

he suffered and was buried;
and the third day he rose again,
according to the Scriptures;
and ascended into heaven,
and sits on the right hand of the Father;
and he shall come again, with glory, to judge the living and the dead;
whose kingdom shall have no end.

And I believe in the Holy Spirit,
the Lord and Giver of life;
who proceeds from the Father and the Son;
who with the Father and the Son together is worshiped and glorified;
who spoke by the prophets.

And I believe in one holy catholic[10]
and apostolic church.
I acknowledge one baptism
for the remission of sins;
and I look for the resurrection of the dead,
and the life of the world to come. Amen.

ENDNOTES

1 "Come, Thou Long Expected Jesus" by Charles Wesley, a wonderful Christmas hymn written in 1744.

2 Spurgeon is drawing from the Nicene Creed: a creed written in the 4th century to defend and articulate the deity of Christ. You can find the full text of the creed in the appendix.

3 From The Nicene Creed.

4 From the hymn "Guide Me, O Thou Great Jehovah," written in 1745 by William Williams. This hymn was then translated from Welsh into English by Peter Williams in 1771.

5 "Hark! the Herald Angels Sing," written by Charles Wesley in 1739 and adapted by George Whitefield in 1753. The hymn was originally titled by Wesley, "Hymn for Christmas-Day." Whitefield's adapted lyrics are used in Spurgeon's quotation, along with Spurgeon adding his own rhyme in the second line.

6 Isaac Watts, "Joy to the World," in The Sing Hymnal (Wheaton: Crossway, 2025), 780. Watts originally wrote this wonderful hymn in 1719.

7 Eternal generation of the Son is a vital Christian doctrine that the Son of God is truly God (from eternity), and has always been the Son of God, one with Father.

8 From the Nicene Creed.

9 See *Creeds, Confessions, and Catechisms: A Reader's Edition*, edited by Chad Van Dixhoorn, (Crossway, 2022), p. 17–18.

10 The word "catholic" means universal—the one church of Christ across all times, places, and people.